LUIGI PIRANDELLO (1867–1936) was born in Kaos near Girgenti, Sicily. He attended the University of Rome and received a doctorate in philology at Bonn University in 1891. Pirandello began his literary career as a poet, but soon turned to fiction and in 1904 published his first widely recognized novel, *The Late Mattia Pascal*. With the appearance of *It Is So!* in 1917, Pirandello proved himself to be one of the most original and powerful dramatists of the twentieth century, a claim well substantiated by his two greatest plays, *Six Characters in Search of an Author* (1921) and *Henry IV* (1922). Pirandello opened his own Art Theatre in Rome in 1925, and was awarded the Nobel Prize in 1934.

ERIC BENTLEY, acclaimed playwright, critic, and translator, edited the standard American volume of Pirandello's plays, *Naked Masks* (1952). Later, he added his *Pirandello Commentaries* (1986) and his own translation of *Pirandello's Major Plays* (1991). He is also General Editor of the Grove Press edition of the works of Bertolt Brecht. Among his critical works are *The Playwright as Thinker* (1946) and *The Life of the Drama* (1964). His plays are published in the collections *Rallying Cries, Monstrous Martyrdoms*, and *The Kleist Variations*.

SIX CHARACTERS IN SEARCH OF AN AUTHOR

by Luigi Pirandello

*English Version and Introduction
by Eric Bentley*

A SIGNET CLASSIC

SIGNET CLASSIC
Published by New American Library, a division of
Penguin Group (USA) Inc., 375 Hudson Street,
New York, New York 10014, USA
Penguin Group (Canada), 10 Alcorn Avenue, Toronto,
Ontario M4V 3B2, Canada (a division of Pearson Penguin Canada Inc.)
Penguin Books Ltd., 80 Strand, London WC2R 0RL, England
Penguin Ireland, 25 St. Stephen's Green, Dublin 2,
Ireland (a division of Penguin Books Ltd.)
Penguin Group (Australia), 250 Camberwell Road, Camberwell, Victoria 3124,
Australia (a division of Pearson Australia Group Pty. Ltd.)
Penguin Books India Pvt. Ltd., 11 Community Centre, Panchsheel Park,
New Delhi - 110 017, India
Penguin Group (NZ), cnr Airborne and Rosedale Roads, Albany,
Auckland 1310, New Zealand (a division of Pearson New Zealand Ltd.)
Penguin Books (South Africa) (Pty.) Ltd., 24 Sturdee Avenue,
Rosebank, Johannesburg 2196, South Africa

Penguin Books Ltd., Registered Offices:
80 Strand, London WC2R 0RL, England

Published by Signet Classic, an imprint of New American Library, a division of
Penguin Group (USA) Inc. This translation is reprinted from *Pirandello's Major
Plays*, translated by Eric Bentley, Northwestern University Press. For informa-
tion, address Abrams Artists Agency: (Fax) 646-486-0100.

First Signet Classic Printing, May 1998

CONTENTS

IN SEARCH OF THIS AUTHOR

1867: born in Kaos near Girgenti (now Agrigento), Sicily
1891: won his doctorate at the University of Bonn
1893: published his first novel, *The Outcast*
1904: published what would be his best-known novel, *The Late Mattia Pascal*
1914–18: began to write plays regularly during World War I
1917: *Right You Are*
1921: *Six Characters in Search of an Author*
1922: *Emperor Henry (Enrico IV)*
1924: *Each in His Own Way*
1926–36: wrote his nine last plays and made a gift of them to Marta Abba. Perhaps the most notable is *Tonight We Improvise*
1934: awarded the Nobel Prize for Literature
1936: died in Rome

Pirandello wrote seven novels, of which the following six have been published, at one time or another, in English: *The Outcast, The Merry-Go-Round of Love, The Late Mattia Pascal, The Old and the Young, Shoot!, One, No One, and One Hundred Thousand.*

He planned to write 365 stories and entitle the result *Stories for One Year,* but only 233 got written. Over the years, beginning in 1932, 10 volumes of Pirandello stories have been published in English: *Horse in the Moon, The Naked Truth, Better Think Twice About It, The Medals, Short Stories* (Simon and Schuster), *The Merry-Go-Round of Love and Selected Stories, Short Stories* (Oxford University Press), *Tales of Madness, Tales of Suicide,* and *Eleven Short Stories.*

In the twenties, Pirandello's plays were published as they appeared by E. P. Dutton in the United States. Most of the nine plays he gave to Marta Abba in the thirties were published by Samuel French. Since 1952, the only published collection of Pirandello's plays to be regularly available in the U.S. has been *Naked Masks* edited by Eric Bentley (Meridian).

A Translator's
Introduction, 1998

It is not often that anything really happens in the history of drama, but at least twice in this our century, now about over, something did. Many of us can remember the second of these occasions: It was the premiere of *Waiting for Godot*, Paris, 1953. The first occasion, before our time maybe, was the premiere of *Six Characters in Search of an Author*, Rome, 1921. Acclaim, on this earlier occasion, was not immediate. The first-night audience just shouted: *"Manicomio!—Madhouse!"* But by 1925 the playwright who had created the *Six Characters* was ready to announce:

> If modesty forbids me to accept George Bernard Shaw's assertion that *Six Characters* is the most original and most powerful work of all the theatres ancient and modern in all nations, I can't help being aware that their appearance in the history of the Italian theatre marks a date that people won't be able to forget.

Well, yes, he was carried away. Shaw had not asserted that. Asked for a comment, Shaw actually said:

> I have no recollection of the extravagant dictum you quote: but I rank P. as first rate among playwrights and have never come across a play so original as *Six Chracters* [sic].

And we know Shaw had "come across" a lot of plays: from Shakespeare to Ibsen—and Shaw.
So original. Not the greatest of plays, perhaps, but the

most original. More original than the *Oresteia* or *Tamburlaine* or *Faust* or *A Doll's House,* to name just four plays that have been considered innovative? Comparative measurement is impossible. Shaw's claim is based, surely, not on precise parallels, but on a sense of the radicality of Pirandello's action in penning this particular script. Was he writing a play at all? And if not, what was this product he called *Six Characters in Search of an Author*? A disquisitory dialogue *about* the writing of plays? A play-in-the-making, to use a Pirandellian phrase, but therefore not made and so: unfinished? A quasi-improvisation of a play? A fantasy founded on the notion that characters are not created by an author, but are preternatural people who seek an author to write their biographies or at least their family drama?

One might go first to Pirandello himself for answers. He provided some. Speaking of this play and two others (*Each in His Own Way* and *Tonight We Improvise*), he wrote:

> . . . the three together . . . form something of a trilogy of the theatre in the theatre, not only because there is action both on the stage and in the auditorium, in a box and in the corridors and in the lobby of a theatre, but also because the whole complex of theatrical elements—characters and actors, author and director, dramatic critics and spectators (external to the action or involved in it)—present every possible conflict.

In these final years of the twentieth century, theatregoers and readers find these features no longer innovative but familiar, yet in the early twenties, audiences were amazed and perhaps dismayed to find, on entering the auditorium, the curtain up and stage work-lights illuminating the (possibly brick) back wall of the theatre. This feature, together with the others listed here in Pirandello's own words, abolished the proscenium arch and therewith a whole host of traditional theatrics coming down through the Victorian theatre from the earlier Baroque. This was, according to a leading American playwright of the thirties and forties, Thornton Wilder, the new theatre, *the* theatre of "our time."

There were scholarly commentators, of a historical

bent, to remark that there is nothing new under the sun, and that Pirandello had merely taken over the play-within-a-play, long ago adopted by Shakespeare in *The Taming of the Shrew* and, in another way, in *Hamlet*; but that is only a pedantic gibe. Nearer to Pirandello are two plays (c. 1800) of the German poet Ludwig Tieck, *Puss in Boots* and *The Land of Upside Down*, in which different orders of being (characters, spectators, writers, et al.) intermingle much more intricately than in the old-fashioned play-within-a-play (of which a fairer example than anything in Shakespeare is Beaumont and Fletcher's *Knight of the Burning Pestle*).

Not even Tieck comes close. If his heterodox form represents more than a technical experiment, it still is only playful. Perhaps it derived from a theory or can be attributed to one in hindsight, but Pirandello's "experiment" is quite other than technical and external, and if he had some pertinent theories, they were thought up later or provided by his admiring critic Adriano Tilgher. My allusion here is to the Preface to the play which Pirandello published in 1925, and even there he states that the play was in no way a premeditated thing: It was a dream play that came to him spontaneously and rapidly, as dreams come: in a series of images, all highly charged, not with philosophy, but with emotion, with passion.

Above all, *Six Characters* was not experimental. No first-rate art is. Experiments belong to science: The scientist decides on a hypothesis and then tests it, knowing that many tests will fail, but that he might make a breakthrough someday. That is not how artists work, and the "experimental forms" of, say, Conrad or Faulkner are really quite *un*experimental: They evolved organically from their authors' original sense of narrative. And so, while *Six Characters* was something that came to his mind quickly, as in a vision, Pirandello had been working toward it for years, as can readily be shown by examination of not only his previous plays, but also his novels and short stories.

If *Six Characters* should not be taken as a technical experiment, what should it be taken as? Or, to focus the question better, if all the features of "theatre in the theatre" are not technical experiments, what are they? Here the answer, in my view, is not the same for *Six Characters* as for the other two plays I have mentioned (or other Pirandello plays I have not mentioned). These other plays can fairly be seen as, to a large extent, *pièces à thèse*: They are structured to prove a point, albeit to prove it quite dramatically and therefore passionately. The final moments of these plays come with the force of Euclid's *Quod erat demonstrandum*. Even so tense and hectic a drama as *Emperor Henry (Enrico IV)* is not an exception.

Six Characters is. And I have always relished the final line of its first version: "So I've wasted a whole day!" says the Director, which might be translated as: So it doesn't amount to a hill of beans. Conclusions anyone? No grand conclusion, certainly. Perhaps no conclusion at all.

Six Characters offers fragments, vignettes, visionary scenes, arranged in a certain order, not by the brains of a craftsman-calculator as in the French well-made play or commercial drama generally, but by intuition, imagination, fancy (call it what you will). The effect is dazzling, and critics have been dazzled. Now when dazzled, you see nothing—but, remembering bits and pieces, you can begin to speculate. There is a body of ideas by now universally denominated "Pirandellian," and here is the Maestro attempting to compress them into half a dozen lines:

> . . . the deceit of mutual understanding irremediably founded on the empty abstraction of words, the multiple personality of everyone (corresponding to the possibilities of being to be found in each of us), and finally the inherent tragic conflict between life (which is always moving and changing) and form (which fixes it, immutable).

And, oh yes, all these messages are delivered, some of them more than once or twice, in *Six Characters*.

Result: A critic has spotted this message or that and declared it The Meaning of *Six Characters in Search of an Author*. Perhaps this idea or that was stated with particular poignancy, and perhaps it had particular significance for this critic or that: He or she had that much justification for seizing on it and brandishing it with enthusiasm: Pirandello the Light Bearer! Which would be fair enough were this an essay offering miscellaneous ideas from which you take your pick. But supposing it is a play, all appearances to the contrary notwithstanding?

Some of the more philosophic commentators have informed us that it isn't a play. Not as we think of plays. We think of plays as Aristotle described them, and as all the dramatists down the centuries since have written them. But Pirandello blew the whistle? No longer would a play be an imitation (mimesis) of an action and of life? It would be not only the medium but the message: The play would imitate *plays* or bog down in its effort to do so?

One could pursue this line of thought (and a dozen related lines of thought) further. Instead I propose the following. Yes, the idea of a play mirroring life does run into trouble with Pirandello because, for him, life is itself a play. Doesn't the actor imitate (i.e., enact) the non-actor, the "real" person? Yes, but for Pirandello, the real person is an actor. "All the world's a stage / And all the men and women merely players." When the work known as *Six Characters in Search of an Author* is performed, the stage becomes more real than the world. Isn't this obvious, and entirely convincing, to the audience? The boards of the theatre are the prior reality, the bits of scenery called for by the Director, quite secondary. Returning to the topic of originality, I should interject here that this was the first play ever written in which the boards of the theatre did not symbolize and represent some other place, some other reality. Think of the prologue to Shakespeare's *Henry V*: Directly or indirectly it defines the norm, for that cockpit did "hold the vasty fields of France," "the very casques that did affright the air at Agincourt" *were* crammed within that "wooden O." How *ab*normal is Signor Pirandello!

What has seemed to some to be mere flash—just fireworks and legerdemain—has its origin in a particular personal and social experience of the author and retains the pain—extreme pain, which is to say, agony, torment—of that experience, however far he proceeds into exemplification and elaboration. Here let me insert, as something more than an obiter dictum, that the art of the drama must always confront human suffering, the greatest dramatists being those who respond most fully to this challenge.

I have been able to note how *Six Characters in Search of*

an Author was produced in Italy, France, Britain, and the
U.S. during the past half century. Most of the productions
I've seen (and this includes some that I've seen lately on
American TV) have been characterized by directorial
brilliance—a factor not irrelevant to Pirandello's way of
seeing things. Yet that heady brilliance (Tyrone Guthrie's,
for instance) turned the show too far toward comedy. It
became a "simply delightful affair"—with lots of clever
choreography as well as well-handled repartee. Human
suffering was absent, or so mildly present as to present
us, the audience, with no pang, not even a twinge.

Twinges and pangs are called for, however, and this
author does all an author can do to help the actors com-
municate them. The particular personal and social experience just mentioned is this. In the Sicilian village culture
from which he came, Pirandello was struck—more than
struck: overwhelmed—by the misery of family life. (He
believed in "family values" but did not feel that many
agreed with him or at any rate that real families often
achieved anything but misery.) He could depict that misery in the straightforward way of the Naturalists à la
Zola, as his early fiction shows, but his growing preoccu-
pation was with the way misery was observed by the
neighbors and with the way being observed not only in-
creased the misery but became itself the pervasive and,
as it were, definitive misery.

Pirandello's *Six Characters* are actors, *en*actors, of a universal family catastrophe. They would like Pirandello
just to present this in a novel or a play. He declines, and
instead watches them—is their first audience. Their second audience is the Director and his troupe of actors.
Their third audience is the reader of this Pirandello
script—or the spectator in Pirandello's theatre. We have
concentric circles here, and this final one, the theatre audience, makes a decisive difference. It changes the nature
of the smaller circles. For a mere reader, the characters
can be accepted as just characters, the actors as just actors, but, for spectators, the characters are actors *playing*
characters, and the acting troupe is actors playing actors.
Which, of course, is a big "Pirandellian" point.

Even the reader catches the main drift: That the deeper
suffering is not the suffering within the family, but the
suffering created by the interaction of family and non-

family, family and director, family and actors. As for the communication of suffering to the theatre audience: This, of course, is a different kind of suffering. The issue has been discussed by philosophers of drama for hundreds of years: How can tragic suffering on stage not give such pain to the audience that they faint or leave the theatre? The answer is that the audience does not suffer as the characters do, but equally relevant here is that, if none of the suffering comes home, and vividly, to the audience, then they are left indifferent or bored. The director may decide to amuse them if he cannot move them, yet in the case of *Six Characters*, that would be to trivialize Pirandello's work and miss the main target.

One of the best critics of *Six Characters*, Pirandello's biographer Gaspare Giudice, has advised against looking for any "main target" in the play. He has pointed out that a dozen main targets have been cited by as many eminent critics, and none is more than a theme mentioned *in* the play (mostly in the Father's speeches): Which is to say that none can justly claim to be the theme *of* the play. Fair enough. The target I have in mind is, however, not one of those themes nor any other theory or thesis: It is deep suffering, not just the suffering of family life, though that is the innermost of the concentric circles, but the suffering brought about by interaction of family with others, with the audience, the various audiences. The world is theatre, but theatre, too, is theatre: We, the spectators at a performance of *Six Characters in Search of an Author*, are not excluded from the suffering, even though we experience it with a difference.

When I saw the play in recent years in more countries than one, I suffered not at all. There was fun (comedy), there was thought (drama of ideas), there was torrential eloquence and pyrotechnic wordplay, but the main target was missed. The performers failed to plumb the depths of suffering, and so the audience not only didn't suffer (in its own appropriate way), it also never learned the full import of the suffering. The suffering in modern drama from Ibsen to Tennessee Williams and Arthur Miller is neurotic suffering: The image is of man as a neurotic. Pirandello has a sense of a suffering that is, so to speak, metaphysical: Man is maladjusted to the universe, and it hurts. That comes too close, perhaps, to being just an idea, and Pirandello never lingered long with "just ideas." He had a sense, not just an idea, of trouble going deeper than neurosis. Psychosis? For lack of a better word one should perhaps accept it, and take a more candid look at the Father in *Six Characters*. He is the man with "all the ideas," *but* it is as a paranoid that he handles them. Even the plain story of his life, told in bare outline, is the tale of a madman. Take his own account of how he handled his marriage and the arrival of their child. His only idea of fatherhood, in practice, is that he should send the baby out to a wet nurse in the country whose milk will be healthier. He seems to think women of humble background produce better milk, but then again he describes his *wife* as being of humble background. He's crazy. And his craziness hovers over everything, for he is the dominant presence of this play. When the first-night audience in 1921 cried, "*Manicomio!—Madhouse!*" they had hit a bull's-eye.

Is the whole family mad, all six of them? Perhaps not. But theirs is a strange aura, is it not? They seem not merely bizarre, but unutterably remote, alien, sad, steeped in mysterious emotion, spooky. The Stepdaughter, a budding femme fatale, seems to have converted a natural hysteria into fanatic parricidal hostility. Mother and Son are gone, far gone. Pirandello can play with the idea that they are undramatizable in that they have retreated so far into their shells, into alienation, that no writer can get to them. And the children! There were never stage children like this before. An infant girl so close to death that all she has to do is lean over and she's dead.* A boy at the talkative and obstreperous age of fourteen who, in this talkiest of plays, never talks, but instead takes out a gun and kills himself. . . .

Talking of originality, nothing is more original in this play than the presentation of the two children. A play which was all dialogue would wipe them out. On stage, in *Six Characters*, they are a constant presence and their silence speaks volumes. And speaks madness. The two

---

*"At the age of five he watched his little brother fall into a wash-basin and drown; he lost his sight at seven." This is from a *New Yorker* article dated September 5, 1997, about Ray Charles. In Pirandello's play, a boy watches his little sister fall into the shallow basin of a fountain and drown. He goes right out of his mind. His eyes glaze.

kids have been traumatized and "struck dumb." Their drama must remain unspoken but, and this is the Pirandellian point, it is *seen*. There is an audience for it: the Son. And what are *his* credentials? He, too, has refused to talk all evening. He, too, has wonderful silences. Which seem to build, as the Mother at last does some of the talking, to, well, what? A culmination, a climax? Pirandello is the playwright of coitus interruptus. The story of the Son breaks off, and the Author *we* are in search of ends his play, at least the carefully reconsidered 1925 version, with a "classic" tableau of Father, Mother, and Son. (The young children are dead. The Stepdaughter is on her way out.)

When the play is over, you may begin to wonder just who and what these six people are. Are they really only "characters in search of an author"? A troublesome question since not all of them seek to do any such searching, and the notion is a fantasy anyway, almost an allegory. Signifying what? That the writer, Luigi Pirandello, often sat in his room at dusk and had the feeling intruders were present, and that they were book or play characters, asking him to write about them and give them context and, with context, orientation and status? Which would make him a real Author like the God of medieval Catholicism, the head of an authoritative, *the* authoritative, hierarchy. But then this was just what he did *not* feel. Quite the contrary. Pirandello is the poet of a post-Nietzschean world in which God, especially *that* God, has been dead for some time. Yes, the Characters have offered him a role, but, no, he cannot play it.

The flat, *un*allegorical truth is opposite to the fantasy. Characters do not really search for him. He, as writer, searches for *them* and, if they exist, he gave them that existence. The fantasy is quite a curious one, is it not? Zany? Should one say: mad? It would mean our play is mad through and through, characters, author, and all. Making the whole thing a disordered phantasmagoria, almost a Walpurgis Night. This thought brings us to the question of structure.

A dream play such as this can seem—and many have found it so—totally unstructured, formless, a string of all too loosely connected images and thoughts: chaos depicted chaotically. Pirandello liked to say he was born in chaos because he really *was* born in a Sicilian spot named Kaos. Fear of chaos—fear that, in Shakespearean phrase, chaos would "come again"—may be said to underlie all his work.

Which has brought friendly scholars to the rescue with a theory that the apparent disorder of *Six Characters* is really a new and different form of order. For more than two thousand years, order in drama had been seen through Aristotelian eyes. Drama presented the imitation (mimesis) of an action and of life: Life had a certain logic to it, and a dramatic action had a beginning, middle, and end. Pirandello can be said to have changed all this in a drama where what is imitated is not life, or an ordered action, but another drama. For what may appear to some to be "life" is actually just another drama, all the world being a stage, and all the men and women merely players. Pirandello (we are being told) has replaced mimesis with "metamimesis."

In this same period, the nineteen-twenties, Bertolt Brecht concluded that *his* plays were non-Aristotelian and would require a brand-new theory of drama—Epic Theatre—to define and justify them.

Did either playwright really need such revisionism? As far as *Six Characters* is concerned, one should not fail to see, behind the seemingly unstructured flow of images and statements, the simplest three-act structure, and, if it is concealed "behind" something, that concealment is fully explained within the play itself: The play of the Six, the play-in-the-making, does not yet have acts, for it is not yet written, just as its characters do not yet have names, but are offering themselves in the standard roles of Mother, Father et al. (Actually, in the dialogue, names are occasionally introduced.)

Three-act plays, turned out by the thousands in Paris, were standard in the nineteenth and early twentieth century. Act One: beginning. Act Two: middle. Act Three: end. Act One: Exposition and Introduction. Act Two: Development on a rising curve, possibly to a big climax and stunning curtain line. Act Three: The Upshot, which, in the tragic tradition was Catastrophe, in the comic tradition, Dénouement. Modern specialty: the Tragicomic ending (somewhere between Catastrophe and Dénouement).

Now this tight, symmetrical construction is just what

the story of the Six does not have. They would expect their author to impose it: That is what authors are for. And though the would-be author on this stage, namely the Director, hopes to impose it, he does not come anywhere near to succeeding. The author who succeeds is Luigi Pirandello, and he does so by locating the action in the interplay between Characters and Actors. This is the drama that is, and oh so carefully, introduced in the first section; carried to a kind of climax (a kind of anticlimax) in the second section, where the scene in the whorehouse is enacted (not quite enacted, is the Pirandellian touch); and developed in the third section to several conclusions (death of the kids, exposure of the son, termination of the experiment by the Director). And there may be said to be a tiny Epilogue—which is also a Prologue—and the story of the Six could now begin again. (I have been using the word "section" because they are not marked as acts except in English translations that take liberties. Their boundaries are quite clearly indicated in Pirandello's stage directions.)

This structural integration yields what Aristotle called unity of action, a feature that his later disciples linked with unity of time and place. All three unities are strictly observed in *Six Characters*, and the unity of place is restricted, well beyond Aristotle's reckoning, to the boards of the theatre we are in. So this most original of plays is, in some important respects, quite traditional. Pirandello was a leading figure in the European avant-garde of the nineteen-twenties—a time, perhaps the only time, when there really *was* an avant-garde. Not the least daring element in his avant-garde imagination was his retention of a traditional Idea of Theatre. Like Jean Giraudoux, he also belonged to a *théâtre d'arrière garde*.

THE AUTHOR'S PREFACE (1925)

It seems like yesterday but is actually many years ago that a nimble little maidservant entered the service of my art. However, she always comes fresh to the job.

She is called Fantasy.

A little puckish and malicious, if she likes to dress in black no one will wish to deny that she is often positively bizarre and no one will wish to believe that she always does everything in the same way and in earnest. She sticks her hand in her pocket, pulls out a cap and bells, sets it on her head, red as a cock's comb, and dashes away. Here today, there tomorrow. And she amuses herself by bringing to my house—since I derive stories and novels and plays from them—the most disgruntled tribe in the world, men, women, children, involved in strange adventures which they can find no way out of; thwarted in their plans; cheated in their hopes; with whom, in short, it is often torture to deal.

Well, this little maidservant of mine, Fantasy, several years ago, had the bad inspiration or ill-omened caprice to bring a family into my house. I wouldn't know where she fished them up or how, but, according to her, I could find in them the subject for a magnificent novel.

I found before me a man about fifty years old, in a dark jacket and light trousers, with a frowning air and ill-natured, mortified eyes; a poor woman in widow's weeds leading by one hand a little girl of four and by the other a boy of rather more than ten; a cheeky and "sexy" girl, also clad in black but with an equivocal and brazen pomp, all atremble with a lively, biting contempt for the mortified old man and for a young fellow of twenty who stood on one side closed in on himself as if he despised them all. In short, the six characters who are seen coming on stage at the beginning of the play. Now one of them and now another—often beating down one another—

embarked on the sad story of their adventures, each shouting his own reasons, and projecting in my face his disordered passions, more or less as they do in the play to the unhappy Manager.

What author will be able to say how and why a character was born in his fantasy? The mystery of artistic creation is the same as that of birth. A woman who loves may desire to become a mother; but the desire by itself, however intense, cannot suffice. One fine day she will find herself a mother without having any precise intimation when it began. In the same way an artist imbibes very many germs of life and can never say how and why, at a certain moment, one of these vital germs inserts itself into his fantasy, there to become a living creature on a plane of life superior to the changeable existence of every day.

I can only say that, without having made any effort to seek them out, I found before me, alive—you could touch them and even hear them breathe—the six characters now seen on the stage. And they stayed there in my presence, each with his secret torment and all bound together by the one common origin and mutual entanglement of their affairs, while I had them enter the world of art, constructing from their persons, their passions, and their adventures a novel, a drama, or at least a story.

Born alive, they wished to live.

To me it was never enough to present a man or a woman and what is special and characteristic about them simply for the pleasure of presenting them; to narrate a particular affair, lively or sad, simply for the pleasure of narrating it; to describe a landscape simply for the pleasure of describing it.

There are some writers (and not a few) who do feel this pleasure and, satisfied, ask no more. They are, to speak more precisely, historical writers.

But there are others who, beyond such pleasure, feel a more profound spiritual need on whose account they admit only figures, affairs, landscapes which have been soaked, so to speak, in a particular sense of life and acquire from it a universal value. These are, more precisely, philosophical writers.

I have the misfortune to belong to these last.

I hate symbolic art in which the presentation loses all spontaneous movement in order to become a machine,

an allegory—a vain and misconceived effort because the
very fact of giving an allegorical sense to a presentation
clearly shows that we have to do with a fable which by itself has no truth either fantastic or direct; it was made for
the demonstration of some moral truth. The spiritual
need I speak of cannot be satisfied—or seldom, and that
to the end of a superior irony, as for example in Ariosto—
by such allegorical symbolism. This latter starts from a
concept, and from a concept which creates or tries to
create for itself an image. The former on the other hand
seeks in the image—which must remain alive and free
throughout—a meaning to give it value.

Now, however much I sought, I did not succeed in un-
covering this meaning in the six characters. And I concluded therefore that it was no use making them live.

I thought to myself: "I have already afflicted my readers
with hundreds and hundreds of stories. Why should I
afflict them now by narrating the sad entanglements of
these six unfortunates?"

And, thinking thus, I put them away from me. Or
rather I did all I could to put them away.

But one doesn't give life to a character for nothing.

Creatures of my spirit, these six were already living a
life which was their own and not mine any more, a life
which it was not in my power any more to deny them.

Thus it is that while I persisted in desiring to drive them
out of my spirit, they, as if completely detached from every
narrative support, characters from a novel miraculously
emerging from the pages of the book that contained them,
went on living on their own, choosing certain moments
of the day to reappear before me in the solitude of my
study and coming—now one, now the other, now two
together—to tempt me, to propose that I present or describe this scene or that, to explain the effects that could be
secured with them, the new interest which a certain unusual situation could provide, and so forth.

For a moment I let myself be won over. And this
condescension of mine, thus letting myself go for a while,
was enough, because they drew from it a new incre-
ment of life, a greater degree of clarity and addition,
consequently a greater degree of persuasive power over
me. And thus as it became gradually harder and harder
for me to go back and free myself from them, it became

easier and easier for them to come back and tempt me. At a certain point I actually became obsessed with them. Until, all of a sudden, a way out of the difficulty flashed upon me.

"Why not," I said to myself, "present this highly strange fact of an author who refuses to let some of his characters live though they have been born in his fantasy, and the fact that these characters, having by now life in their veins, do not resign themselves to remaining excluded from the world of art? They are detached from me; live on their own; have acquired voice and movement; have by themselves—in this struggle for existence that they have had to wage with me—become dramatic characters, characters that can move and talk on their own initiative; already see themselves as such; have learned to defend themselves against me; will even know how to defend themselves against others. And so let them go where dramatic characters do go to have life: on a stage. And let us see what will happen."

That's what I did. And, naturally, the result was what it had to be: a mixture of tragic and comic, fantastic and realistic, in a humorous situation that was quite new and infinitely complex, a drama which is conveyed by means of the characters, who carry it within them and suffer it, a drama, breathing, speaking, self-propelled, which seeks at all costs to find the means of its own presentation; and the comedy of the vain attempt at an improvised realization of the drama on stage. First, the surprise of the poor actors in a theatrical company rehearsing a play by day on a bare stage (no scenery, no flats). Surprise and incredulity at the sight of the six characters announcing themselves as such in search of an author. Then, immediately afterwards, through that sudden fainting fit of the Mother veiled in black, their instinctive interest in the drama of which they catch a glimpse in her and in the other members of the strange family, an obscure, ambiguous drama, coming about so unexpectedly on a stage that is empty and unprepared to receive it. And gradually the growth of this interest to the bursting forth of the contrasting passions of Father, of Step-Daughter, of Son, of that poor Mother, passions seeking, as I said, to overwhelm each other with a tragic, lacerating fury.

And here is the universal meaning at first vainly

sought in the six characters, now that, going on stage of their own accord, they succeed in finding it within themselves in the excitement of the desperate struggle which each wages against the other and all wage against the Manager and the actors, who do not understand them.

Without wanting to, without knowing it, in the strife of their bedevilled souls, each of them, defending himself against the accusations of the others, expresses as his own living passion and torment the passion and torment which for so many years have been the pangs of my spirit: the deceit of mutual understanding irremediably founded on the empty abstraction of the words, the multiple personality of everyone corresponding to the possibilities of being to be found in each of us, and finally the inherent tragic conflict between life (which is always moving and changing) and form (which fixes it, immutable).

Two above all among the six characters, the Father and the Step-Daughter, speak of that outrageous unalterable fixity of their form in which he and she see their essential nature expressed permanently and immutably, a nature that for one means punishment and for the other revenge; and they defend it against the factitious affectations and unaware volatility of the actors, and they try to impose it on the vulgar Manager who would like to change it and adapt it to the so-called exigencies of the theatre.

If the six characters don't all seem to exist on the same plane, it is not because some are figures of first rank and others of the second, that is, some are main characters and others minor ones—the elementary perspective necessary to all scenic or narrative art—nor is it that any are not completely created—for their purpose. They are all six at the same point of artistic realization and on the same level of reality, which is the fantastic level of the whole play. Except that the Father, the Step-Daughter, and also the Son are realized as mind; the Mother as nature; the Boy as a presence watching and performing a gesture and the Baby unaware of it all. This fact creates among them a perspective of a new sort. Unconsciously I had had the impression that some of them needed to be fully realized (artistically speaking), others less so, and others merely sketched in as elements in a narrative or presentational sequence: the most alive, the most completely created, are the Father and the Step-Daughter who naturally stand out more and lead the way, dragging themselves along beside the almost dead weight of the others—first, the Son, holding back; second, the Mother, like a victim resigned to her fate, between the two children who have hardly any substance beyond their appearance and who need to be led by the hand.

And actually! actually they had each to appear in that stage of creation which they had attained in the author's fantasy at the moment when he wished to drive them away.

If I now think about these things, about having intuited that necessity, having unconsciously found the way to resolve it by means of a new perspective, and about the way in which I actually obtained it, they seem like miracles. The fact is that the play was really conceived in one of those spontaneous illuminations of the fantasy when by a miracle all the elements of the mind answer to each other's call and work in divine accord. No human brain, working "in the cold," however stirred up it might be, could ever have succeeded in penetrating far enough, could ever have been in a position to satisfy all the exigencies of the play's form. Therefore the reasons which I will give to clarify the values of the play must not be thought of as intentions that I conceived beforehand when I prepared myself for the job and which I now undertake to defend, but only as discoveries which I have been able to make afterwards in tranquillity.

I wanted to present six characters seeking an author. Their play does not manage to get presented—precisely because the author whom they seek is missing. Instead is presented the comedy of their vain attempt with all that it contains of tragedy by virtue of the fact that the six characters have been rejected.

But can one present a character while rejecting him? Obviously, to present him one needs, on the contrary, to receive him into one's fantasy before one can express him. And I have actually accepted and realized the six characters: I have, however, accepted and realized them as rejected: in search of *another* author.

What have I rejected of them? Not themselves, obviously, but their drama, which doubtless is what interests them above all but which did not interest me—for the reasons already indicated.

And what is it, for a character—his drama?

Every creature of fantasy and art, in order to exist, must have his drama, that is, a drama in which he may be a character and for which he *is* a character. This drama is the character's *raison d'être*, his vital function, necessary for his existence.

In these six, then, I have accepted the "being" without the reason for being. I have taken the organism and entrusted to it, not its own proper function, but another more complex function into which its own function entered, if at all, only as a datum. A terrible and desperate situation especially for the two—Father and Step-Daughter—who more than the others crave life and more than the others feel themselves to be characters, that is, absolutely need a drama and therefore their own drama—the only one which they can envisage for themselves yet which meantime they see rejected: an "impossible" situation from which they feel they must escape at whatever cost; it is a matter of life and death. True, I have given them another *raison d'être*, another function: precisely that "impossible" situation, the drama of being in search of an author and rejected. But that this should be a *raison d'être*, that it should have become their real function, that it should be necessary, that it should suffice, they can hardly suppose; for they have a life of their own. If someone were to tell them, they wouldn't believe him. It is not possible to believe that the sole reason for our living should lie in a torment that seems to us unjust and inexplicable.

I cannot imagine, therefore, why the charge was brought against me that the character of the Father was not what it should have been because it stepped out of its quality and position as a character and invaded at times the author's province and took it over. I who understand those who don't quite understand me see that the charge derives from the fact that the character expresses and makes his own a torment of spirit which is recognized as mine. Which is entirely natural and of absolutely no significance. Aside from the fact that this torment of spirit in the character of the Father derives from causes, and is suffered and lived for reasons, that have nothing to do with the drama of my personal experience, a fact which alone removes all substance from the criticism, I want to make it clear that the inherent torment of my spirit is one thing, a torment which I can legitimately—provided that it be organic—reflect in a character, and that the activity of my spirit as revealed in the realized work, the activity that succeeds in forming a drama out of the six characters in search of an author is another thing. If the Father participated in this latter activity, if he competed in forming the drama of the six characters without an author, then and only then would it by all means be justified to say that he was at times the author himself and therefore not the man he should be. But the Father suffers and does not create his existence as a character in search of an author. He suffers it as an inexplicable fatality and as a situation which he tries with all his powers to rebel against, which he tries to remedy: hence it is that he is a character in search of an author and nothing more, even if he expresses as his own the torment of my spirit. If he, so to speak, assumed some of the author's responsibilities, the fatality would be completely explained. He would, that is to say, see himself accepted, if only as a rejected character, accepted in the poet's heart of hearts, and he would no longer have any reason to suffer the despair of not finding someone to construct and affirm his life as a character. I mean that he would quite willingly accept the *raison d'être* which the author gives him and without regrets would forego his own, throwing over the Manager and the actors to whom in fact he runs as his only recourse.

There is one character, that of the Mother, who on the other hand does not care about being alive (considering being alive as an end in itself). She hasn't the least suspicion that she is *not* alive. It has never occurred to her to ask how and why and in what manner she lives. In short, she is not aware of being a character, inasmuch as she is never, even for a moment, detached from her role. She doesn't know she has a role.

This makes her perfectly organic. Indeed, her role of Mother does not of itself, in its natural essence, embrace mental activity. And she does not exist as a mind. She lives in an endless continuum of feeling, and therefore she cannot acquire awareness of her life—that is, of her existence as a character. But with all this, even she, in her own way and for her own ends, seeks an author, and at a certain stage seems happy to have been brought before the Manager. Because she hopes to take life from him, perhaps? No: because she hopes the Manager will have her present a scene with the Son in which she would put so much of her own life. But it is a scene which does not exist, which never has and never could take place. So unaware is she of being a character, that is, of the life that is possible to her, all fixed and determined, moment by moment, in every action, every phrase.

She appears on stage with the other characters but without understanding what the others make her do. Obviously, she imagines that the itch for life with which the husband and the daughter are afflicted and for which she herself is to be found on stage is no more than one of the usual incomprehensible extravagances of this man who is both tortured and torturer and—horrible, most horrible—a new equivocal rebellion on the part of that poor erring girl. The Mother is completely passive. The events of her own life and the values they assume in her eyes, her very character, are all things which are "said" by the others and which she only once contradicts, and that because the maternal instinct rises up and rebels within her to make it clear that she didn't at all wish to abandon either the son or the husband: the Son was taken from her and the husband forced her to abandon him. She is only correcting data; she explains and knows nothing.

In short, she is nature. Nature fixed in the figure of a mother.

This character gave me a satisfaction of a new sort, not to be ignored. Nearly all my critics, instead of defining her, after their habit, as "unhuman"—which seems to be the peculiar and incorrigible characteristic of all my creatures without exception—had the goodness to note "with real pleasure" that at last a *very human* figure had emerged from my fantasy. I explain this praise to myself in the following way: since my poor Mother is entirely limited to the natural attitude of a Mother with no possibility of free mental activity, being, that is, little more than a lump of flesh completely alive in all its functions—procreation, lactation, caring for and loving its young—without any need therefore of exercising her brain, she realizes in her person the true and complete "human type." That must be how it is, since in a human organism nothing seems more superfluous than the mind.

But the critics have tried to get rid of the Mother with

this praise without bothering to penetrate the nucleus of poetic values which the character in the play represents. A very human figure, certainly, because mindless, that is, unaware of being what she is or not caring to explain it to herself. But not knowing that she is a character doesn't prevent her from being one. That is her drama in my play. And the most living expression of it comes spurting out in her cry to the Manager who wants her to think all these things have happened already and therefore cannot now be a reason for renewed lamentations: "No, it's happening now, it's happening always! My torture is not a pretence, signore! I am alive and present, always, in every moment of my torture: it is renewed, alive and present, always!" This she *feels*, without being conscious of it, and feels it therefore as something inexplicable: but she feels it so terribly that she doesn't think it *can* be something to explain either to herself or to others. She feels it and that is that. She feels it as pain, and this pain is immediate; she cries it out. Thus she reflects the growing fixity of life in a form—the same thing, which in another way, tortures the Father and the Step-Daughter. In them, mind. In her, nature. The mind rebels and, as best it may, seeks an advantage; nature, if not aroused by sensory stimuli, weeps.

Conflict between life-in-movement and form is the inexorable condition not only of the mental but also of the physical order. The life which in order to exist has become fixed in our corporeal form little by little kills that form. The tears of a nature thus fixed lament the irreparable, continuous aging of our bodies. Hence the tears of the Mother are passive and perpetual. Revealed in three faces, made significant in three distinct and simultaneous dramas, this inherent conflict finds in the play its most complete expression. More: the Mother declares also the particular value of artistic form—a form which does not delimit or destroy its own life and which life does not consume—in her cry to the Manager. If the Father and Step-Daughter began their scene a hundred thousand times in succession, always, at the appointed moment, at the instant when the life of the work of art must be expressed with that cry, it would always be heard, unaltered and unalterable in its form, not as a mechanical repetition, not as a return determined by external necessities, but on the contrary, alive every time and as new, suddenly born *thus forever!* embalmed alive in its incorruptible form. Hence, always, as we open the book, we shall find Francesca alive and confessing to Dante her sweet sin, and if we turn to the passage a hundred thousand times in succession, a hundred thousand times in succession Francesca will speak her words, never repeating them mechanically, but saying them as though each time were the first time with such living and sudden passion that Dante every time will turn faint. All that lives, by the fact of living, has a form, and by the same token must die—except the work of art which lives forever in so far as it *is* form.

The birth of a creature of human fantasy, a birth which is a step across the threshold between nothing and eternity, can also happen suddenly, occasioned by some necessity. An imagined drama needs a character who does or says a certain necessary thing; accordingly this character is born and is precisely what he had to be. In this way Madame Pace is born among the six characters and seems a miracle, even a trick, realistically portrayed on the stage. It is no trick. The birth is real. The new character is alive not because she was alive already but because she is now happily born as is required by the fact of her being a character—she is obliged to be as she is. There is a break here, a sudden change in the level of reality of the scene, because a character can be born in this way only in the poet's fancy and not on the boards of a stage. Without anyone's noticing it, I have all of a sudden changed the scene: I have gathered it up again into my own fantasy without removing it from the spectator's eyes. That is, I have shown them, instead of the stage, my own fantasy in the act of creating—my own fantasy in the form of this same stage. The sudden and uncontrollable changing of a visual phenomenon from one level of reality to another is a miracle comparable to those of the saint who sets his own statue in motion: it is neither wood nor stone at such a moment. But the miracle is not arbitrary. The stage—a stage which accepts the fantastic reality of the six characters—is no fixed, immutable datum. Nothing in this play exists as given and preconceived. Everything is in the making, is in motion, is a sudden experiment: even the place in which this unformed life, reaching after its own form, changes and changes again contrives to shift position organically. The level of reality changes. When I had the idea of bringing Madame Pace to birth right there on the stage, I felt I could do it and I did it. Had I noticed that this birth was unhinging and silently, unnoticed, in a second, giving another shape, another reality to my scene, I certainly wouldn't have brought it about. I would have been afraid of the apparent lack of logic. And I would have committed an ill-omened assault on the beauty of my work. The fervor of my mind saved me from doing so. For, despite appearances, with their specious logic, this fantastic birth is sustained by a real necessity in mysterious, organic relation with the whole life of the work.

That someone now tells me it hasn't all the value it could have because its expression is not constructed but chaotic, because it smacks of romanticism, makes me smile.

I understand why this observation was made to me: because in this work of mine the presentation of the drama in which the six characters are involved appears tumultuous and never proceeds in an orderly manner. There is no logical development, no concatenation of the events. Very true. Had I hunted it with a lamp I couldn't have found a more disordered, crazy, arbitrary, complicated, in short, romantic way of presenting "the drama in which the six characters are involved." Very true. But I have not presented that drama. I have presented another—and I won't undertake to say again what!—in which, among the many fine things that everyone, according to his tastes, can find, there is a discreet satire on romantic procedures: in the six characters thus excited to the point where they stifle themselves in the roles which each of them plays in a certain drama while I present them as characters in another play which they don't know and don't suspect the existence of, so that this inflammation of their passions—which belongs to the realm of romantic procedures—is humorously "placed," located in the void. And the drama of the six characters presented not as it would have been organized by my fantasy had it been accepted but in this way, as a rejected drama, could not exist in the work except as a "situation," with some little development, and could not come out except in indications, stormily, disorderedly, in violent foreshortenings, in a chaotic manner: continually interrupted, sidetracked, contradicted (by one of its characters), denied, and (by two others) not even seen.

There is a character indeed—he who denies the drama which makes him a character, the Son—who draws all his importance and value from being a character not of the comedy in the making—which as such hardly appears—but from the presentation that I made of it. In short, he is the only one who lives solely as "a character in search of an author"—inasmuch as the author he seeks is not a dramatic author. Even this could not be otherwise. The character's attitude is an organic product of my conception, and it is logical that in the situation it should produce greater confusion and disorder and another element of romantic contrast.

But I had precisely to *present* this organic and natural chaos. And to present a chaos is not at all to present chaotically, that is, romantically. That my presentation is the reverse of confused, that it is quite simple, clear, and orderly, is proved by the clarity which the intrigue, the characters, the fantastic and realistic, dramatic and comic levels of the work have had for every public in the world and by the way in which, for those with more searching vision, the unusual values enclosed within it come out.

Great is the confusion of tongues among men if criticisms thus made find words for their expression. No less great than this confusion is the intimate law of order which, obeyed in all points, makes this work of mine classical and typical and at its catastrophic close forbids the use of words. Though the audience eventually understands that one does not create life by artifice and that the drama of the six characters cannot be presented without an author to give them value with his spirit, the Manager remains vulgarly anxious to know how the thing turned out, and the "ending" is remembered by the Son in its sequence of actual moments, but without any sense and therefore not needing a human voice for its expression. It happens stupidly, uselessly, with the going-off of a mechanical weapon on stage. It breaks up and disperses the sterile experiment of the characters and the actors, which has apparently been made without the assistance of the poet.

The poet, unknown to them, as if looking on at a distance during the whole period of the experiment, was at the same time busy creating—with it and of it—his own play.

(Translated E.B. 1950)

SIX CHARACTERS
IN SEARCH OF
AN AUTHOR

CHARACTERS OF THE PLAY-IN-THE-MAKING

The Father
The Mother
The Son, aged 22
The Stepdaughter, 18

The Boy, 14
The Little Girl, 4
    (these two last do not
    speak)
Then, called into being:
    Madam Pace

ACTORS IN THE COMPANY

The Director (Direttore-
    Capocomico)
Leading Lady
Leading Man
Second Actress
Ingenue
Juvenile Lead
Other actors and actresses

Stage Manager
Prompter
Property Man
Technician
Director's Secretary
Stage Door Man
Stage Crew

THE PLACE: *The stage of a playhouse.*

The play has neither acts nor scenes. The performance should be interrupted twice: first—without any lowering of the curtain—when
the Director and the chief among the Characters retire to put the sce-
nario together and the Actors leave the stage; second when the Technician lets the curtain down by mistake.

When the audience arrives in the theater, the curtain is raised; and the stage, as normally in the daytime, is without wings or scenery and almost completely dark and empty. From the beginning we are to receive the impression of an unrehearsed performance.

Two stairways, left and right respectively, connect the stage with the auditorium.

On stage the dome of the prompter's box has been placed on one side of the box itself. On the other side, at the front of the stage, a small table and an armchair with its back to the audience, for the DIRETTORE-CAPOCOMICO [DIRECTOR].

Two other small tables of different sizes with several chairs around them have also been placed at the front of the stage, ready as needed for the rehearsal. Other chairs here and there, left and right, for the actors, and at the back, a piano, on one side and almost hidden.

As soon as the houselights dim, the TECHNICIAN is seen entering at the door on stage. He is wearing a blue shirt, and a tool bag hangs from his belt. From a corner at the back he takes several stage braces, then arranges them on the floor downstage, and kneels down to hammer some nails in. At the sound of the hammering, the STAGE MANAGER comes running from the door that leads to the dressing rooms.

STAGE MANAGER. Oh! What are you doing?
TECHNICIAN. What am I doing? Hammering.
STAGE MANAGER. At this hour? [He looks at the clock] It's ten-thirty already. The Director will be here any moment. For the rehearsal.
TECHNICIAN. I gotta have time to work, too, see.
STAGE MANAGER. You will have. But not now.
TECHNICIAN. When?
STAGE MANAGER. Not during rehearsal hours. Now

move along, take all this stuff away, and let me set
the stage for the second act of, um, *The Game of Role
Playing.*

[*Muttering, grumbling, the* TECHNICIAN *picks up the
stage braces and goes away. Meanwhile, from the door on
stage, the* ACTORS OF THE COMPANY *start coming in, both
men and women, one at a time at first, then in twos, at ran-
dom, nine or ten of them, the number one would expect as
the cast in rehearsals of Pirandello's play "The Game of
Role Playing,"[1] which is the order of the day. They enter,
greet the* STAGE MANAGER *and each other, all saying good-
morning to all. Several go to their dressing rooms. Others,
among them the* PROMPTER, *who has a copy of the script
rolled up under his arm, stay on stage, waiting for the* DI-
RECTOR *to begin the rehearsal. Meanwhile, either seated
in conversational groups, or standing, they exchange a few
words among themselves. One lights a cigarette, one complains about the part he has been assigned, one reads aloud
to his companions items of news from a theater journal. It
would be well if both the Actresses and the Actors wore
rather gay and brightly colored clothes and if this first improvised scene* [scena a soggetto] *combined vivacity with
naturalness. At a certain point, one of the actors can sit
down at the piano and strike up a dance tune. The younger
actors and actresses start dancing.*]

STAGE MANAGER [*clapping his hands to call them to order*].
   All right, that's enough of that. The Director's here.

[*The noise and the dancing stop at once. The Actors turn
and look toward the auditorium from the door of which the*
DIRECTOR *is now seen coming. A bowler hat on his head, a
walking stick under his arm, and a big cigar in his mouth,
he walks down the aisle and, greeted by the Actors, goes on
stage by one of the two stairways. The* SECRETARY *hands
him his mail: several newspapers and a script in a wrapper.*]

DIRECTOR. Letters?

SECRETARY. None. That's all the mail there is.

DIRECTOR [*handing him the script*]. Take this to my room. [*Then, looking around and addressing himself to the* STAGE MANAGER] We can't see each other in here. Want to give us a little light?

STAGE MANAGER. OK.

[*He goes to give the order, and shortly afterward, the whole left side of the stage where the Actors are is lit by a vivid white light. Meanwhile, the* PROMPTER *has taken up his position in his box. He uses a small lamp and has the script open in front of him.*]

DIRECTOR [*clapping his hands*]. Very well, let's start. [*To the* STAGE MANAGER] Someone missing?

STAGE MANAGER. The Leading Lady.

DIRECTOR. As usual! [*He looks at the clock*] We're ten minutes late already. Fine her for that, would you, please? Then she'll learn to be on time.

[*He has not completed his rebuke when the voice of the* LEADING LADY *is heard from the back of the auditorium.*]

LEADING LADY. No, no, for Heaven's sake! I'm here! I'm here! [*She is dressed all in white with a big, impudent hat on her head and a cute little dog in her arms. She runs down the aisle and climbs one of the sets of stairs in great haste.*]

DIRECTOR. You've sworn an oath always to keep people waiting.

LEADING LADY. You must excuse me. Just couldn't find a taxi. But you haven't even begun, I see. And I'm not on right away. [*Then, calling the* STAGE MANAGER *by name, and handing the little dog over to him*] Would you please shut him in my dressing room?

DIRECTOR [*grumbling*]. And the little dog to boot! As if

there weren't enough dogs around here. [*He claps his hands again and turns to the* PROMPTER.] Now then, the second act of *The Game of Role Playing*. [*As he sits down in his armchair*] Quiet, gentlemen. Who's on stage?

[*The Actresses and Actors clear the front of the stage and go and sit on one side, except for the three who will start the rehearsal and the* LEADING LADY *who, disregarding the* DIRECTOR's *request, sits herself down at one of the two small tables.*]

DIRECTOR [*to the* LEADING LADY]. You're in this scene, are you?

LEADING LADY. Me? No, no.

DIRECTOR [*irritated*]. Then how about getting up, for Heaven's sake?

[*The* LEADING LADY *rises and goes and sits beside the other Actors who have already gone to one side.*]

DIRECTOR [*to the* PROMPTER]. Start, start.

PROMPTER [*reading from the script*]. "In the house of Leone Gala. A strange room, combined study and dining room."

DIRECTOR [*turning to the* STAGE MANAGER]. We'll use the red room.

STAGE MANAGER [*making a note on a piece of paper*]. Red room. Very good.

PROMPTER [*continuing to read from the script*]. "The table is set and the desk has books and papers on it. Shelves with books on them, and cupboards with lavish tableware. Door in the rear through which one goes to Leone's bedroom. Side door on the left through which one goes to the kitchen. The main entrance is on the right."

DIRECTOR [*rising and pointing*]. All right, now listen

carefully. That's the main door. This is the way to the kitchen. [*Addressing himself to the Actor playing the part of Socrates*] You will come on and go out on this side. [*To the* STAGE MANAGER] The compass at the back. And curtains. [*He sits down again.*]

STAGE MANAGER [*making a note*]. Very good.

PROMPTER [*reading as before*]. "Scene One. Leone Gala, Guido Venanzi, Filippo called Socrates." [*To the* DIRECTOR] Am I supposed to read the stage directions, too?

DIRECTOR. Yes, yes, yes! I've told you that a hundred times!

PROMPTER [*reading as before*]. "At the rise of the curtain, Leone Gala, wearing a chef's hat and apron, is intent on beating an egg in a saucepan with a wooden spoon. Filippo, also dressed as a cook, is beating another egg. Guido Venanzi, seated, is listening."

LEADING ACTOR [*to the* DIRECTOR]. Excuse me, but do I really have to wear a chef's hat?

DIRECTOR [*annoyed by this observation*]. I should say so! It's in the script. [*And he points at it.*]

LEADING ACTOR. But it's ridiculous, if I may say so.

DIRECTOR [*leaping to his feet, furious*]. "Ridiculous, ridiculous!" What do you want me to do? We never get a good play from France any more, so we're reduced to producing plays by Pirandello, a fine man and all that, but neither the actors, the critics, nor the audience are ever happy with his plays, and if you ask me, he does it all on purpose. [*The Actors laugh. And now he rises and coming over to the* LEADING ACTOR *shouts:*] A cook's hat, yes, my dear man! And you beat eggs. And you think you have nothing more on your hands than the beating of eggs? Guess again. You symbolize the shell of those eggs. [*The Actors resume their laughing, and start making ironical comments among themselves.*] Silence! And pay attention while I explain. [*Again addressing himself to the*

LEADING ACTOR] Yes, the shell: that is to say, the empty *form* of reason without the *content* of instinct, which is blind. You are reason, and your wife is instinct in the game of role playing. You play the part assigned you, and you're your own puppet—of your own free will. Understand?

LEADING ACTOR [*extending his arms, palms upward*]. Me? No.

DIRECTOR [*returning to his place*]. Nor do I. Let's go on. Wait and see what I do with the ending. [*In a confidential tone*] I suggest you face three-quarters front. Otherwise, what with the abstruseness of the dialogue, and an audience that can't hear you, good-bye play! [*Again clapping*] Now, again, order! Let's go.

PROMPTER. Excuse me, sir, may I put the top back on the prompter's box? There's rather a draft.

DIRECTOR. Yes, yes, do that.

[*The STAGE DOOR MAN has entered the auditorium in the meanwhile, his braided cap on his head. Proceeding down the aisle, he goes up on stage to announce to the DIRECTOR the arrival of the Six Characters, who have also entered the auditorium, and have started following him at a certain distance, a little lost and perplexed, looking around them.*

Whoever is going to try and translate this play into scenic terms must take all possible measures not to let these Six Characters get confused with the Actors of the Company. Placing both groups correctly, in accordance with the stage directions, once the Six are on stage, will certainly help, as will lighting the two groups in contrasting colors. But the most suitable and effective means to be suggested here is the use of special masks for the Characters: masks specially made of material which doesn't go limp when sweaty and yet masks which are not too heavy for the Actors wearing them, cut out and worked over so they leave eyes, nostrils, and mouth free. This will also bring out the inner significance of the play. The Characters in fact should not be presented as ghosts but as created realities, unchanging constructs of the imagination, and therefore more solidly real than the Actors with their fluid naturalness. The masks will help to give the impression of figures constructed by art, each one unchangeably fixed in the expression of its own fundamental sentiment, thus:

remorse *in the case of the* FATHER; revenge *in the case of the* STEPDAUGHTER; disdain *in the case of the* SON; grief *in the case of the* MOTHER, who should have wax tears fixed in the rings under her eyes and on her cheeks, as with the sculpted and painted images of the mater dolorosa in church. Their clothes should be of special material and design, without extravagance, with rigid, full folds like a statue, in short not suggesting a material you might buy at any store in town, cut out and tailored at any dressmaker's.

The FATHER *is a man of about fifty, hair thin at the temples, but not bald, thick mustache coiled round a still youthful mouth that is often open in an uncertain, pointless smile. Pale, most notably on his broad forehead; blue eyes, oval, very clear and piercing; dark jacket and light trousers; at times gentle and smooth, at times he has hard, harsh outbursts.*

The MOTHER *seems scared and crushed by an intolerable weight of shame and self-abasement. Wearing a thick black crepe widow's veil, she is modestly dressed in black, and when she lifts the veil, the face does not show signs of suffering, and yet seems made of wax. Her eyes are always on the ground.*

The STEPDAUGHTER, *eighteen, is impudent, almost insolent. Very beautiful, and also in mourning, but mourning of a showy elegance. She shows contempt for the timid, afflicted, almost humiliated manner of her little brother, rather a mess of a* BOY, *fourteen, also dressed in black, but a lively tenderness for her little sister, a* LITTLE GIRL *of around four, dressed in white with black silk sash round her waist.*

The SON, *twenty-two, tall, almost rigid with contained disdain for the* FATHER *and supercilious indifference toward the* MOTHER, *wears a mauve topcoat and a long green scarf wound round his neck.*]

STAGE DOOR MAN [*beret in hand*]. Excuse me, your honor.

DIRECTOR [*rudely jumping on him*]. What is it now?

STAGE DOOR MAN [*timidly*]. There are some people here asking for you.

[*The* DIRECTOR *and the Actors turn in astonishment to look down into the auditorium.*]

DIRECTOR [*furious again*]. But I'm rehearsing here! And you know perfectly well no one can come in during rehearsal! [*Turning again toward the house*] Who are these people? What do they want?

THE FATHER [*stepping forward, followed by the others, to one of the two little stairways to the stage*]. We're here in search of an author.

DIRECTOR [*half angry, half astounded*]. An author? What author?

FATHER. Any author, sir.

DIRECTOR. There's no author here at all. It's not a new play we're rehearsing.

STEPDAUGHTER [*very vivaciously as she rushes up the stairs*]. Then so much the better, sir! *We* can be your new play!

ONE OF THE ACTORS [*among the racy comments and laughs of the others*]. Did you hear that?

FATHER [*following the* STEPDAUGHTER *onstage*]. Certainly, but if the author's not here ... [*to the* DIRECTOR] Unless *you'd* like to be the author?

[*The* MOTHER, *holding the* LITTLE GIRL *by the hand, and the* BOY *climb the first steps of the stairway and remain there waiting. The* SON *stays morosely below.*]

DIRECTOR. Is this your idea of a joke?

FATHER. Heavens, no! Oh, sir, on the contrary: we bring you a painful drama.

STEPDAUGHTER. We can make your fortune for you.

DIRECTOR. Do me a favor, and leave. We have no time to waste on madmen.

FATHER [*wounded, smoothly*]. Oh, sir, you surely know that life is full of infinite absurdities which, brazenly enough, do not need to appear probable, because they're true.

DIRECTOR. What in God's name are you saying?

FATHER. I'm saying it can actually be considered madness, sir, to force oneself to do the opposite: that is, to give probability to things so they will seem true. But permit me to observe that, if this is madness, it is also the *raison d'être* of your profession.

[*The Actors become agitated and indignant.*]

DIRECTOR [*rising and looking him over*]. It is, is it? It seems to you an affair for madmen, our profession?

FATHER. Well, to make something seem true which is not true ... without any need, sir: just for fun ... Isn't it your job to give life on stage to creatures of fantasy?

DIRECTOR [*immediately, making himself spokesman for the growing indignation of his Actors.*] Let me tell you something, my good sir. The actor's profession is a very noble one. If, as things go nowadays, our new playwrights give us nothing but stupid plays, with puppets in them instead of men, it is our boast, I'd have you know, to have given life—on these very boards—to immortal works of art.

[*Satisfied, the Actors approve and applaud their* DIRECTOR.]

FATHER [*interrupting and bearing down hard*]. Exactly! That's just it. You have created living beings—*more* alive than those that breathe and wear clothes! Less real, perhaps; but more true! We agree completely!

[*The Actors look at each other, astounded.*]

DIRECTOR. What? You were saying just now ...
FATHER. No, no, don't misunderstand me. You shouted that you hadn't time to waste on madmen. So I wanted to tell you that no one knows better than you that Nature employs the human imagination to carry her work of creation on to a higher plane!
DIRECTOR. All right, all right. But what are you getting at, exactly?
FATHER. Nothing, sir. I only wanted to show that one may be born to this life in many modes, in many forms: as tree, as rock, water or butterfly ... or woman. And that ... characters are born too.
DIRECTOR [*his amazement ironically feigned*]. And you— with these companions of yours—were born a character?
FATHER. Right, sir. And alive, as you see.

[*The DIRECTOR and the Actors burst out laughing as at a joke.*]

FATHER [*wounded*]. I'm sorry to hear you laugh, be- cause, I repeat, we carry a painful drama within us, as you all might deduce from the sight of that lady there, veiled in black.

[*As he says this, he gives his hand to the MOTHER to help her up the last steps and, still holding her by the hand, he leads her with a certain tragic solemnity to the other side of the stage, which is suddenly bathed in fantastic light. The LITTLE GIRL and the BOY follow the MOTHER; then the SON,*] *who stands on one side at the back; then the* STEPDAUGHTER *who also detaches herself from the others—downstage and leaning against the proscenium arch. At first astonished at this development, then overcome with admiration, the Actors now burst into applause as at a show performed for their benefit.*]

DIRECTOR [*bowled over at first, then indignant*]. Oh, stop this! Silence please! [*Then, turning to the Characters*] And you, leave! Get out of here! [*To the* STAGE MANAGER] For God's sake, get them out!

STAGE MANAGER [*stepping forward but then stopping, as if held back by a strange dismay*]. Go! Go!

FATHER [*to the* DIRECTOR]. No, look, we, um—

DIRECTOR [*shouting*]. I tell you we've got to work!

LEADING MAN. It's not right to fool around like this . . .

FATHER [*resolute, stepping forward*]. I'm amazed at your incredulity! You're accustomed to seeing the created characters of an author spring to life, aren't you, right here on this stage, the one confronting the other? Perhaps the trouble is there's no script *there* [*pointing to the* PROMPTER'S *box*] with us in it?

STEPDAUGHTER [*going right up to the* DIRECTOR, *smiling, coquettish*]. Believe me, we really are six characters, sir. Very interesting ones at that. But lost. Adrift.

FATHER [*brushing her aside*]. Very well: lost, adrift. [*Going right on*] In the sense, that is, that the author who created us, made us live, did not wish, or simply and materially was not able, to place us in the world of art. And that was a real crime, sir, because whoever has the luck to be born a living character can also laugh at death. He will never die! The man will die, the writer, the instrument of creation; the creature will never die! And to have eternal life it doesn't even take extraordinary gifts, nor the performance of miracles. Who was Sancho Panza? Who was Don Abbondio?[2] But they live forever because, as live germs, they have the luck to find a fertile matrix, an imagination which knew how to raise and nourish them, make them live through all eternity!

DIRECTOR. That's all well and good. But what do you people want here?

FATHER. We want to live, sir.

DIRECTOR [*ironically*]. Through all eternity?

FATHER. No, sir. But for a moment at least. In you.

AN ACTOR. Well, well, well!

LEADING LADY. They want to live in us.

JUVENILE LEAD [*pointing to the* STEPDAUGHTER]. Well, I've no objection, so long as I get that one.

FATHER. Now look, look. The play is still in the making. [*To the* DIRECTOR] But if you wish, and your actors wish, we can make it right away. Acting in concert.

LEADING MAN [*annoyed*]. Concert? We don't put on concerts! We do plays, dramas, comedies!

FATHER. Very good. That's why we came.

DIRECTOR. Well, where's the script?

FATHER. Inside us, sir. [*The Actors laugh.*] The drama is inside us. It *is* us. And we're impatient to perform it. According to the dictates of the passion within us.

STEPDAUGHTER [*scornful, with treacherous grace, deliberate impudence*]. My passion—if you only knew, sir! My passion—for him! [*She points to the* FATHER *and makes as if to embrace him but then breaks into a strident laugh.*]

FATHER [*an angry interjection*]. You keep out of this now. And please don't laugh that way!

STEPDAUGHTER. No? Then, ladies and gentlemen, permit me. A two months' orphan, I shall dance and sing for you all. Watch how! [*She mischievously starts to sing "Beware of Chu Chin Chow" by Dave Stamper, reduced to fox trot or slow one-step by Francis Salabert: the first verse, accompanied by a step or two of dancing.*[3] *While she sings and dances, the Actors, especially the* young ones, as if drawn by some strange fascination, move toward her and half raise their hands as if to take hold of her. She runs away and when the Actors burst into applause she just stands there, remote, abstracted, while the DIRECTOR protests.]

ACTORS AND ACTRESSES [*laughing and clapping*]. Brava! Fine! Splendid!

DIRECTOR [*annoyed*]. Silence! What do you think this is, a night spot? [*Taking the FATHER a step or two to one side, with a certain amount of consternation*] Tell me something. Is she crazy?

FATHER. Crazy? Of course not. It's much worse than that.

STEPDAUGHTER [*running over at once to the DIRECTOR*]. Worse! Worse! Not crazy but worse! Just listen: I'll play it for you right now, this drama, and at a certain point you'll see me—when this dear little thing—[*She takes the LITTLE GIRL who is beside the MOTHER by the hand and leads her to the DIRECTOR.*]—isn't she darling? [*Takes her in her arms and kisses her.*] Sweetie! Sweetie! [*Puts her down again and adds with almost involuntary emotion.*] Well, when God suddenly takes this little sweetheart away from her poor mother, and that idiot there—[*thrusting the BOY forward, rudely seizing him by a sleeve*] does the stupidest of things, like the nitwit that he is, [*with a shove she drives him back toward the MOTHER*] then you will see me take to my heels. Yes, ladies and gentlemen, take to my heels! I can hardly wait for that moment. For after what happened between him and me—[*She points to the FATHER with a horrible wink.*] something very intimate, you understand—I can't stay in such company any longer, witnessing the anguish of our mother on account of that fool there—[*She points to the SON.*] Just look at him, look at him!—how indifferent, how frozen, because he is the legitimate son, that's what he is, full of contempt

for me, for him [*the* BOY], and for that little creature
[*the* LITTLE GIRL], because we three are bastards,
d'you see? bastards. [*Goes to the* MOTHER *and embraces her.*] And this poor mother, the common
mother of us all, he—well, he doesn't want to ac-
knowledge her as *his* mother too, and he looks
down on her, that's what he does, looks on her as
only the mother of us three bastards, the wretch!
[*She says this rapidly in a state of extreme excitement.
Her voice swells to the word: "bastards!" and descends
again to the final "wretch," almost spitting it out.*]

MOTHER [*to the* DIRECTOR, *with infinite anguish*]. In the
name of these two small children, sir, I implore
you . . . [*She grows faint and sways.*] Oh, heavens . . .

FATHER [*rushing over to support her with almost all the
Actors who are astonished and scared*]. Please! Please, a
chair, a chair for this poor widow!

ACTORS [*rushing over*].—Is it true then?—She's *really*
fainting?

DIRECTOR. A chair!

[*One of the Actors proffers a chair. The others stand around,
ready to help. The* MOTHER, *seated, tries to stop the* FATHER
from lifting the veil that hides her face.]

FATHER [*to the* DIRECTOR]. Look at her, look at her . . .

MOTHER. Heavens, no, stop it!

FATHER. Let them see you. [*He lifts her veil.*]

MOTHER [*rising and covering her face with her hands, desperate*]. Oh, sir, please stop this man from carrying
out his plan. It's horrible for me!

DIRECTOR [*surprised, stunned*]. I don't know where
we're at! What's this all about? [*To the* FATHER] Is
this your wife?

FATHER [*at once*]. Yes, sir, my wife.

DIRECTOR. Then how is she a widow, if you're alive?

[*The Actors relieve their astonishment in a loud burst of laughter.*]

FATHER [*wounded, with bitter resentment*]. Don't laugh! Don't laugh like that! Please! Just that is her drama, sir. She had another man. Another man who should be here!

MOTHER [*with a shout*]. No! No!

STEPDAUGHTER. He had the good luck to die. Two months ago, as I told you. We're still in mourning, as you see.

FATHER. But he's absent, you see, not just because he's dead. He's absent—take a look at her, sir, and you will understand at once!—Her drama wasn't in the love of two men for whom she was incapable of feeling anything—except maybe a little gratitude [not to me, but to him]—She is not a woman, she is a mother!—And her drama—a powerful one, very powerful—is in fact all in those four children which she bore to her two men.

MOTHER. *My* men? Have you the gall to say I wanted two men? It was him, sir. He forced the other man on me. Compelled—yes, compelled—me to go off with him!

STEPDAUGHTER [*cutting in, roused*]. It's not true!

MOTHER [*astounded*]. How d'you mean, not true?

STEPDAUGHTER. It's not true! It's not true!

MOTHER. And what can you know about it?

STEPDAUGHTER. It's not true. [*To the* DIRECTOR] Don't believe it. Know why she says it? For his sake. [*Pointing to the* SON] His indifference tortures her, destroys her. She wants him to believe that, if she abandoned him when he was two, it was because he [*the* FATHER] compelled her to.

MOTHER [*with violence*]. He did compel me, he did compel me, as God is my witness! [*To the* DIRECTOR] Ask him if that isn't true. [*Her husband*] Make him

tell him. [*The* SON] She couldn't know anything
about it.

STEPDAUGHTER. With my father, while he lived, I know
you were always happy and content. Deny it if
you can.

MOTHER. I don't deny it, I don't . . .

STEPDAUGHTER. He loved you, he cared for you! [*To the*
BOY, *with rage*] Isn't that so? Say it! Why don't you
speak, you dope?

MOTHER. Leave the poor boy alone. Why d'you want
to make me out ungrateful, daughter? I have no
wish to offend your father! I told him [*the* FATHER] I
didn't abandon my son and my home for my own
pleasure. It wasn't my fault.

FATHER. That's true, sir. It was mine.

[*Pause*]

LEADING MAN [*to his companions*]. What a show!

LEADING LADY. And *they* put it on—for us.

JUVENILE LEAD. Quite a change!

DIRECTOR [*who is now beginning to get very interested*].
Let's listen to this, let's listen! [*And saying this, he
goes down one of the stairways into the auditorium, and
stands in front of the stage, as if to receive a spectator's
impression of the show.*]

SON [*without moving from his position, cold, quiet, ironic*].
Oh yes, you can now listen to the philosophy lecture.
He will tell you about the Demon of Experiment.

FATHER. You are a cynical idiot, as I've told you a hundred times. [*To the* DIRECTOR, *now in the auditorium*]
He mocks me, sir, on account of that phrase I found
to excuse myself with.

SON [*contemptuously*]. Phrases!

FATHER. Phrases! Phrases! As if they were not a comfort to everyone: in the face of some unexplained

fact, in the face of an evil that eats into us, to find a word that says nothing but at least quiets us down!

STEPDAUGHTER. Quiets our guilt feelings too. That above all.

FATHER. Our guilt feelings? Not so. I have never quieted my guilt feelings with words alone.

STEPDAUGHTER. It took a little money as well, didn't it, it took a little dough! The hundred lire he was going to pay me, ladies and gentlemen!

[*Movement of horror among the Actors.*]

SON [*with contempt toward the* STEPDAUGHTER]. That's filthy.

STEPDAUGHTER. Filthy? The dough was there. In a small pale blue envelope on the mahogany table in the room behind the shop. Madam Pace's [*she pronounces it "Pah-chay"*] shop. One of those Madams who lure us poor girls from good families into their *ateliers* under the pretext of selling *Robes et Manteaux*.

SON. And with those hundred lire he was going to pay she has bought the right to tyrannize over us all. Only it so happens—I'd have you know—that he never actually incurred the debt.

STEPDAUGHTER. Oh, oh, but we were really going to it, I assure you! [*She bursts out laughing.*]

MOTHER [*rising in protest*]. Shame, daughter! Shame!

STEPDAUGHTER. [*quickly*]. Shame? It's my revenge! I am frantic, sir, frantic to live it, live that scene! The room . . . here's the shopwindow with the coats in it; there's the bed-sofa; the mirror; a screen; and in front of the window the little mahogany table with the hundred lire in the pale blue envelope. I can see it. I could take it. But you men should turn away now: I'm almost naked. I don't blush any more. It's he that blushes now. [*Points to the* FATHER.] But I assure you he was very pale, very pale, at that moment. [*To the* DIRECTOR] You must believe me, sir.

DIRECTOR. You lost me some time ago.

FATHER. Of course! Getting it thrown at you like that! Restore a little order, sir, and let *me* speak. And never mind this ferocious girl. She's trying to heap opprobrium on me by withholding the relevant explanations!

STEPDAUGHTER. This is no place for longwinded narratives!

FATHER. I said—explanations.

STEPDAUGHTER. Oh, certainly. Those that suit your turn.

[*At this point, the* DIRECTOR *returns to the stage to restore order.*]

FATHER. But that's the whole root of the evil. Words. Each of us has, inside him, a world of things—to everyone, his world of things. And how can we understand each other, sir, if, in the words I speak, I put the sense and value of things as they are inside me, whereas the man who hears them inevitably receives them in the sense and with the value they have for him, the sense and value of the world inside him? We think we understand each other but we never do. Consider: the compassion, all the compassion I feel for this woman [*the* MOTHER] has been received by her as the most ferocious of cruelties!

MOTHER. You ran me out of the house.

FATHER. Hear that? Ran her out. It *seemed to her* that I ran her out.

MOTHER. You can talk; I can't . . . But, look, sir, after he married me . . . and who knows why he did? I was poor, of humble birth . . .

FATHER. And that's why. I married you for your . . . humility. I loved you for it, believing . . . [*He breaks off, seeing her gestured denials; seeing the impossibility of*

*making himself understood by her, he opens his arms
wide in a gesture of despair, and turns to the* DIRECTOR]
See that? She says No. It's scarifying, isn't it, sir,
scarifying, this deafness of hers, this mental deafness! She has a heart, oh yes, where her children are
concerned! But she's deaf, deaf in the brain, deaf, sir,
to the point of desperation!

STEPDAUGHTER [*to the* DIRECTOR]. All right, but now
make him tell you what his intelligence has ever
done for us.

FATHER. If we could only foresee all the evil that can
result from the good we believe we're doing!

[*At this point, the* LEADING LADY, *who has been on hot
coals seeing the* LEADING MAN *flirt with the* STEPDAUGHTER,
steps forward and asks of the DIRECTOR:]

LEADING LADY: Excuse me, is the rehearsal continuing?
DIRECTOR. Yes, of course! But let me listen a moment.
JUVENILE LEAD. This is something quite new.
INGENUE. Very interesting!
LEADING LADY. If that sort of thing interests you. [*And
she darts a look at the* LEADING MAN.]
DIRECTOR [*to the* FATHER]. But you must give us *clear*
explanations. [*He goes and sits down.*]
FATHER. Right. Yes. Listen. There was a man work-
ing for me. A poor man. As my secretary. Very de-
voted to me. Understood *her* [*the* MOTHER] very well.
There was mutual understanding between them.
Nothing wrong in it. They thought no harm at
all. Nothing off-color about it. No, no, he knew his
place, as she did. They didn't do anything wrong.
Didn't even think it.

STEPDAUGHTER. So he thought it *for* them. And did it.
FATHER. It's not true! I wanted to do them some good.
And myself too, oh yes, I admit. I'd got to this point,
sir: I couldn't say a word to either of them but they

would exchange a significant look. The one would
consult the eyes of the other, asking how what I had
said should be taken, if they didn't want to put me
in a rage. That sufficed, you will understand, to
keep me continually in a rage, in a state of unbearable exasperation.

DIRECTOR. Excuse me, why didn't you fire him, this
secretary?

FATHER. Good question! That's what I did do, sir. But
then I had to see that poor woman remain in my
house, a lost soul. Like an animal without a master
that one takes pity on and carries home.

MOTHER. No, no, it's—

FATHER [*at once, turning to her to get it in first*]. Your
son? Right?

MOTHER. He'd already snatched my son from me.

FATHER. But not from cruelty. Just so he'd grow up
strong and healthy. In touch with the soil.

STEPDAUGHTER [*pointing at the latter, ironic*]. And just
look at him!

FATHER [*at once*]. Uh? Is it also my fault if he then grew
up this way? I sent him to a wet nurse, sir, in the
country, a peasant woman. I didn't find her [*the*
MOTHER] strong enough, despite her humble origin.
I'd married her for similar reasons, as I said. All
nonsense maybe, but there we are. I always had
these confounded aspirations toward a certain solidity, toward what is morally sound. [*Here the* STEP-
DAUGHTER *bursts out laughing.*] Make her stop that!
It's unbearable!

DIRECTOR. Stop it. I can't hear, for Heaven's sake!

[*Suddenly, again, as the* DIRECTOR *rebukes her, she is withdrawn and remote, her laughter cut off in the middle. The*
DIRECTOR *goes down again from the stage to get an impression of the scene.*]

FATHER. I couldn't bear to be with that woman any more. [*Points to the* MOTHER] Not so much, believe me, because she irritated me, and even made me feel physically ill, as because of the pain—a veritable anguish—that I felt on her account.

MOTHER. And he sent me away!

FATHER. Well provided for. And to that man. Yes, sir. So she could be free of me.

MOTHER. And so *he* could be free.

FATHER. That, too. I admit it. And much evil resulted. But I intended good. And more for her than for me, I swear it! [*He folds his arms across his chest. Then, suddenly, turning to the* MOTHER] I never lost sight of you, never lost sight of you till, from one day to the next, unbeknown to me, he carried you off to another town. He noticed I was interested in her, you see, but that was silly, because my interest was absolutely pure, absolutely without ulterior motive. The interest I took in her new family, as it grew up, had an unbelievable tenderness to it. Even she should bear witness to that! [*He points to the* STEPDAUGHTER.]

STEPDAUGHTER. Oh, very much so! I was a little sweetie. Pigtails over my shoulders. Panties coming down a little bit below my skirt. A little sweetie. He would see me coming out of school, at the gate. He would come and see me as I grew up . . .

FATHER. This is outrageous. You're betraying me!

STEPDAUGHTER. I'm not! What do you mean?

FATHER. Outrageous. Outrageous. [*Immediately, still excited, he continues in a tone of explanation, to the* DIRECTOR.] My house, sir, when she had left it, at once seemed empty. [*Points to the* MOTHER] She was an incubus. But she filled my house for me. Left alone, I wandered through these rooms like a fly without a head. This fellow here [*the* SON] was raised away from home. Somehow, when he got back, he didn't seem mine any more. Without a mother between me and him, he grew up on his own, apart, without any relationship to me, emotional or intellectual. And then—strange, sir, but true—first I grew curious, then I was gradually attracted toward *her* family, which I had brought into being. The thought of *this* family began to fill the void around me. I had to— really had to—believe she was at peace, absorbed in the simplest cares of life, lucky to be away and far removed from the complicated torments of my spirit. And to have proof of this, I would go and see that little girl at the school gate.

STEPDAUGHTER. Correct! He followed me home, smiled at me and, when I was home, waved to me, like this! I would open my eyes wide and look at him suspiciously. I didn't know who it was. I told mother. And she guessed right away it was him. [*The* MOTHER *nods.*] At first she didn't want to send me back to school for several days. When I did go, I saw him again at the gate—the clown!—with a brown paper bag in his hand. He came up to me, caressed me, and took from the bag a lovely big Florentine straw hat with a ring of little May roses round it— for me!

DIRECTOR. You're making too long a story of this.

SON [*contemptuously*]. Story is right! Fiction! Literature!

FATHER. Literature? This is life, sir. Passion!

DIRECTOR. Maybe! But not actable!

FATHER. I agree. This is all preliminary. I wouldn't *want* you to act it. As you see, in fact, she [*the* STEP-DAUGHTER] is no longer that little girl with pigtails—

STEPDAUGHTER. —and the panties showing below her skirt!

FATHER. The drama comes now, sir. Novel, complex—

STEPDAUGHTER [*gloomy, fierce, steps forward*].—What my father's death meant for us was—

FATHER [*not giving her time to continue*].—poverty, sir.

They returned, unbeknownst to me. She's so thick-headed. [*Pointing to the* MOTHER] It's true she can hardly write herself, but she could have had her daughter write, or her son, telling me they were in need!

MOTHER. But, sir, how could I have guessed he felt the way he did?

FATHER. Which is just where you always went wrong. You could never guess how I felt about anything!

MOTHER. After so many years of separation, with all that had happened . . .

FATHER. And is it my fault if that fellow carried you off as he did? [*Turning to the* DIRECTOR] From one day to the next, as I say. He'd found some job someplace. I couldn't even trace them. Necessarily, then, my interest dwindled, with the years. The drama breaks out, sir, unforeseen and violent, at their return. When I, alas, was impelled by the misery of my still living flesh . . . Oh, and what misery that is for a man who is alone, who has not wanted to form debasing relationships, not yet old enough to do without a woman, and no longer young enough to go and look for one without shame! Misery? It's horror, horror, because no woman can give him love any more.— Knowing this, one should go without! Well, sir, on the outside, when other people are watching, each man is clothed in dignity: but, on the inside, he knows what unconfessable things are going on within him. One gives way, gives way to temptation, to rise again, right afterward, of course, in a great hurry to put our dignity together again, complete, solid, a stone on a grave that hides and buries from our eyes every sign of our shame and even the very memory of it! It's like that with everybody. Only the courage to say it is lacking—to say certain things.

STEPDAUGHTER. The courage to do them, though—everybody's got that.

FATHER. Everybody. But in secret. That's why it takes more courage to say them. A man only has to say them and it's all over: he's labeled a cynic. But, sir, he isn't! He's just like everybody else. Better! He's better because he's not afraid to reveal, by the light of intelligence, the red stain of shame, there, in the human beast, which closes its eyes to it. Woman—yes, woman—what is she like, actually? She looks at us, inviting, tantalizing. You take hold of her. She's no sooner in your arms than she shuts her eyes. It is the sign of her submission. The sign with which she tells the man: Blind yourself for I am blind.

STEPDAUGHTER. How about when she no longer keeps them shut? When she no longer feels the need to hide the red stain of shame from herself by closing her eyes, and instead, her eyes dry now and impassive, sees the shame of the man, who has blinded himself even without love? They make me vomit, all those intellectual elaborations, this philosophy that begins by revealing the beast and then goes on to excuse it and save its soul . . . I can't bear to hear about it! Because when a man feels obliged to *reduce* life this way, reduce it all to "the beast," throwing overboard every vestige of the truly human, every aspiration after chastity, all feelings of purity, of the ideal, of duties, of modesty, of shame, then nothing is more contemptible, more nauseating than his wretched guilt feelings! Crocodile tears!

DIRECTOR. Let's get to the facts, to the facts! This is just discussion.

FATHER. Very well. But a fact is like a sack. When it's empty, it won't stand up. To make it stand up you must first pour into it the reasons and feelings by which it exists. I couldn't know that—when that man died and they returned here in poverty—she went out to work as a dressmaker to support the children, nor that the person she went to work for was that . . . that Madam Pace!

STEPDAUGHTER. A highclass dressmaker, if you'd all like to know! To all appearances, she serves fine ladies, but then she arranges things so that the fine ladies serve *her* . . . without prejudice to ladies not so fine!

MOTHER. Believe me, sir, I never had the slightest suspicion that that old witch hired me because she had her eye on my daughter . . .

STEPDAUGHTER. Poor mama! Do you know, sir, what the woman did when I brought her my mother's work? She would point out to me the material she'd ruined by giving it to my mother to sew. And she deducted for that, she deducted. And so, you understand, *I* paid, while that poor creature thought she was making sacrifices for me and those two by sewing, even at night, Madam Pace's material!

[*Indignant movements and exclamations from the Actors.*]

DIRECTOR [*without pause*]. And there, one day, you met—

STEPDAUGHTER [*pointing to the* FATHER].—him, him, yes sir! An old client! Now there's a scene for you to put on! Superb!

FATHER. Interrupted by her—the mother—

STEPDAUGHTER [*without pause, treacherously*].—almost in time!—

FATHER [*shouting*]. No, no, *in* time! Because, luckily, I recognized the girl in time. And I took them all back, sir, into my home. Now try to visualize my situation and hers, the one confronting the other— she as you see her now, myself unable to look her in the face any more.

STEPDAUGHTER. It's too absurd! But—afterward— was it possible for me to be a modest little miss, virtuous and well-bred, in accordance with those confounded aspirations toward a certain solidity, toward what is morally sound?

FATHER. And therein lies the drama, sir, as far as I'm concerned: in my awareness that each of us thinks of himself as *one* but that, well, it's not true, each of us is many, oh so many, sir, according to the possibilities of being that are in us. We are one thing for this person, another for that. Already *two* utterly different things! And with it all, the illusion of being always one thing for all men, and always this one thing in every single action. It's not true! Not true! We realize as much when, by some unfortunate chance, in one or another of our acts, we find ourselves suspended, hooked. We see, I mean, that we are not wholly in that act, and that therefore it would be abominably unjust to judge us by that act alone, to hold us suspended, hooked, in the pillory, our whole life long, as if our life were summed up in that act! Now do you understand this girl's treachery? She surprised me in a place, in an act, in which she should never have had to know me—I couldn't be that way for her. And she wants to give me a reality such as I could never have expected I would have to assume for her, the reality of a fleeting moment, a shameful one, in my life! This, sir, this is what I feel most strongly. And you will see that the drama will derive tremendous value from this. But now add the situation of the others! His ... [*He points to the* SON.]

SON [*shrugging contemptuously*]. Leave me out of this! It's none of my business.

FATHER. What? None of your business?

SON. None. And I *want* to be left out. I wasn't made to be one of you, and you know it.

STEPDAUGHTER. We're common, aren't we?—And he's so refined.—But from time to time I give him a hard, contemptuous look, and he looks down at the ground. You may have noticed that, sir. He looks down at the ground. For he knows the wrong he's done me.

SON [*hardly looking at her*]. Me?

STEPDAUGHTER. You! You! I'm on the streets because of you! [*A movement of horror from the Actors*] Did you or did you not, by your attitude, deny us—I won't say the intimacy of home but even the hospitality which puts guests at their ease? We were the intruders, coming to invade the kingdom of your legitimacy! I'd like to have you see, sir, certain little scenes between just him and me! He says I tyrannized over them all. But it was entirely because of his attitude that I started to exploit the situation he calls filthy, a situation which had brought me into his home with my mother, who is also *his* mother, *as its mistress!*

SON [*coming slowly forward*]. They can't lose, sir, three against one, an easy game. But figure to yourself a son, sitting quietly at home, who one fine day sees a young woman arrive, an impudent type with her nose in the air, asking for his father, with whom she has heaven knows what business; and then he sees her return, in the same style, accompanied by that little girl over there; and finally he sees her treat his father—who can say why?—in a very ambiguous and cool manner, demanding money, in a tone that takes for granted that he *has* to give it, has to, is obligated—

FATHER. —but I *am* obligated: it's for your mother!

SON. How would I know? When, sir, [*to the* DIRECTOR] have I ever seen her? When have I ever heard her spoken of. One day I see her arrive with her, [*the* STEPDAUGHTER] with that boy, with that little girl. They say to me: "It's your mother too, know that?" I manage to figure out from her carryings-on [*pointing at the* STEPDAUGHTER] why they arrived in our

home from one day to the next ... What I'm feeling and experiencing I can't put into words, and
wouldn't want to. I wouldn't want to confess it,
even to myself. It cannot therefore result in any action on my part. You can see that. Believe me, sir,
I'm a character that, dramatically speaking, remains
unrealized. I'm out of place in their company. So
please leave me out of it all!

FATHER. What? But it's just because you're so—

SON [*in violent exasperation*].—I'm so what? How would
you know? When did you ever care about me?

FATHER. *Touché! Touché!* But isn't even that a dramatic
situation? This withdrawnness of yours, so cruel to
me, and to your mother who, on her return home is
seeing you almost for the first time, a grown man
she doesn't recognize, though she knows you're her
son ... [*Pointing out the* MOTHER *to the* DIRECTOR]
Just look at her, she's crying.

STEPDAUGHTER [*angrily, stamping her foot*]. Like the fool
she is!

FATHER [*pointing her out to the* DIRECTOR]. And she can't
abide him, you know. [*Again referring to the* SON]—
He says it's none of his business. The truth is he's almost the pivot of the action. Look at that little boy,
clinging to his mother all the time, scared, humiliated ... It's all because of *him*. [*the* SON] Perhaps the
most painful situation of all is that little boy's: he
feels alien, more than all the others, and the poor little thing is so mortified, so anguished at being taken
into our home—out of charity, as it were ... [*Confi-
dentially*] He's just like his father: humble, doesn't
say anything ...

DIRECTOR. He won't fit anyway. You've no idea what a
nuisance children are on stage.

FATHER. But he wouldn't be a nuisance for long. Nor
would the little girl, no, she's the first to go ...[4]

DIRECTOR. Very good, yes! The whole thing interests me very much indeed. I have a hunch, a definite hunch, that there's material here for a fine play!

STEPDAUGHTER [*trying to inject herself*]. With a character like me in it!

FATHER [*pushing her to one side in his anxiety to know what the* DIRECTOR *will decide*]. You be quiet!

DIRECTOR [*going right on, ignoring the interruption*]. Yes, it's new stuff . . .

FATHER. Very new!

DIRECTOR. You had some gall, though, to come and throw it at me this way . . .

FATHER. Well, you see, sir, born as we are to the stage . . .

DIRECTOR. You're amateurs, are you?

FATHER. No. I say: "born to the stage" because . . .

DIRECTOR. Oh, come on, you must have done some acting!

FATHER. No, no, sir, only as every man acts the part assigned to him—by himself or others—in this life. In me you see passion itself, which—in almost all people, as it rises—invariably becomes a bit theatrical . . .

DIRECTOR. Well, never mind! Never mind about that! —You see, my dear sir, without the author . . . I could direct you to an author . . .

FATHER. No, no, look: you be the author!

DIRECTOR. Me? What are you talking about?

FATHER. Yes, you. You. Why not?

DIRECTOR. Because I've never been an author, that's why not!

FATHER. Couldn't you be one now, hm? There's nothing to it. Everyone's doing it. And your job is made all the easier by the fact that you have us—here—alive—right in front of your nose!

DIRECTOR. It wouldn't be enough.

FATHER. Not enough? Seeing us live our own drama . . .

DIRECTOR. I know, but you always need someone to write it!

FATHER. No. Just someone to take it down, maybe, since you have us here—in action—scene by scene. It'll be enough if we piece together a rough sketch for you, then you can rehearse it.

DIRECTOR [*tempted, goes up on stage again*]. Well, I'm almost, almost tempted . . . Just for kicks . . . We could actually rehearse . . .

FATHER. Of course you could! What scenes you'll see emerge! I can list them for you right away.

DIRECTOR. I'm tempted . . . I'm tempted . . . Let's give it a try . . . Come to my office. [*Turns to the Actors*] Take a break, will you? But don't go away. We'll be back in fifteen or twenty minutes. [*To the* FATHER] Let's see what we can do . . . Maybe we can get something very extraordinary out of all this . . .

FATHER. We certainly can. Wouldn't it be better to take *them* along? [*He points to the Characters.*]

DIRECTOR. Yes, let them all come. [*Starts going off, then comes back to address the Actors*] Now don't forget. Everyone on time. Fifteen minutes.

[DIRECTOR *and Six Characters cross the stage and disappear. The Actors stay there and look at one another in amazement.*]

LEADING MAN. Is he serious? What's he going to do?

JUVENILE. This is outright insanity.

A THIRD ACTOR. We have to improvise a drama right off the bat?

JUVENILE LEAD. That's right. Like Commedia dell'Arte.

LEADING LADY. Well, if he thinks *I'm* going to lend myself to that sort of thing . . .

INGENUE. Count me out.

A FOURTH ACTOR [*alluding to the Characters*]. I'd like to know who those people are.

THE THIRD ACTOR. Who would they be? Madmen or crooks!

JUVENILE LEAD. And he's going to pay attention to them?

INGENUE. Carried away by vanity! Wants to be an author now . . .

LEADING MAN. It's out of this world. If this is what the theater is coming to, my friends . . .

A FIFTH ACTOR. I think it's rather fun.

THE THIRD ACTOR. Well! We shall see. We shall see. [*And chatting thus among themselves, the Actors leave the stage, some using the little door at the back, others returning to their dressing rooms.*]

The curtain remains raised. The performance is interrupted by a twenty-minute intermission.

Bells ring. The performance is resumed.[5]

From dressing rooms, from the door, and also from the house, the Actors, the STAGE MANAGER, *the* TECHNICIAN, *the* PROMPTER, *the* PROPERTY MAN *return to the stage; at the same time the* DIRECTOR *and the Six Characters emerge from the office.*

As soon as the house lights are out, the stage lighting is as before.

DIRECTOR. Let's go, everybody! Is everyone here? Quiet! We're beginning. [*Calls the* TECHNICIAN *by name.*]

TECHNICIAN. Here!

DIRECTOR. Set the stage for the parlor scene. Two wings and a backdrop with a door in it will do, quickly please!

[*The* TECHNICIAN *at once runs to do the job, and does it while the* DIRECTOR *works things out with the* STAGE

MANAGER, *the* PROPERTY MAN, *the* PROMPTER, *and the*
Actors. *This indication of a set consists of two wings, a drop
with a door in it, all in pink and gold stripes.*]

DIRECTOR [*to the* PROPERTY MAN]. See if we have some
sort of bed-sofa in the prop room.

PROPERTY MAN. Yes, sir, there's the green one.

STEPDAUGHTER. No, no, not green! It was yellow, flowered, plush, and very big. Extremely comfortable.

PROPERTY MAN. Well, we have nothing like that.

DIRECTOR. But it doesn't matter. Bring the one you have.

STEPDAUGHTER. Doesn't matter? Madam Pace's fa-
mous chaise longue!

DIRECTOR. This is just for rehearsal. Please don't med-
dle! [*To the* STAGE MANAGER] See if we have a display
case—long and rather narrow.

STEPDAUGHTER. The table, the little mahogany table
for the pale blue envelope!

STAGE MANAGER [*to the* DIRECTOR]. There's the small
one. Gilded.

DIRECTOR. All right. Get that one.

FATHER. A large mirror.

STEPDAUGHTER. And the screen. A screen, please, or
what'll I do?

STAGE MANAGER. Yes, ma'am, we have lots of screens,
don't worry.

DIRECTOR [*to the* STEPDAUGHTER]. A few coat hangers?

STEPDAUGHTER. A great many, yes.

DIRECTOR [*to the* STAGE MANAGER]. See how many
we've got, and have them brought on.

STAGE MANAGER. Right, sir, I'll see to it.

[*The* STAGE MANAGER *also hurries to do his job and while
the* DIRECTOR *goes on talking with the* PROMPTER *and then
with the Characters and the Actors, has the furniture carried on by stagehands and arranges it as he thinks fit.*]

DIRECTOR [*to the* PROMPTER]. Meanwhile you can get into position. Look: this is the outline of the scenes, act by act. [*He gives him several sheets of paper.*] You'll have to be a bit of a virtuoso today.

PROMPTER. Shorthand?

DIRECTOR. [*pleasantly surprised*]. Oh, good! You know shorthand?

PROMPTER. I may not know prompting, but shorthand . . . [*Turning to a stagehand*] Get me some paper from my room—quite a lot—all you can find!

[*The stagehand runs off and returns a little later with a wad of paper which he gives to the* PROMPTER.]

DIRECTOR [*going right on, to the* PROMPTER]. Follow the scenes line by line as we play them, and try to pin down the speeches, at least the most important ones. [*Then, turning to the Actors*] Clear the stage please, everyone! Yes, come over to this side and pay close attention. [*He indicates the left.*]

LEADING LADY. Excuse me but—

DIRECTOR [*forestalling*]. There'll be no improvising, don't fret.

LEADING MAN. Then what are we to do?

DIRECTOR. Nothing. For now, just stop, look, and listen. Afterward you'll be given written parts. Right now we'll rehearse. As best we can. With them doing the rehearsing for us. [*He points to the Characters.*]

FATHER [*amid all the confusion on stage, as if he'd fallen from the clouds*]. We're rehearsing? How d'you mean?

DIRECTOR. Yes, for them. You rehearse for them. [*Indicates the Actors.*]

FATHER. But if we are the characters . . .

DIRECTOR. All right, you're characters, but, my dear sir, characters don't perform here, actors perform here. The characters are there, in the script [*He points to the* PROMPTER'S *box.*]—when there *is* a script!

FATHER. Exactly! Since there isn't, and you gentlemen have the luck to have them right here, alive in front of you, those characters . . .

DIRECTOR. Oh, great! Want to do it all yourselves? Appear before the public, do the acting yourselves?

FATHER. Of course. Just as we are.

DIRECTOR [*ironically*]. I'll bet you'd put on a splendid show!

LEADING MAN. Then what's the use of staying?

DIRECTOR [*without irony, to the Characters*]. Don't run away with the idea that you can act! That's laughable . . . [*And in fact the Actors laugh.*] Hear that? They're laughing. [*Coming back to the point*] I was forgetting. I must cast the show. It's quite easy. It casts itself. [*To the* SECOND ACTRESS] You, ma'am, will play the Mother. [*To the* FATHER] You'll have to find her a name.

FATHER. Amalia, sir.

DIRECTOR. But that's this lady's real name. We wouldn't want to call her by her real name!

FATHER. Why not? If that is her name . . . But of course, if it's to be this lady . . . [*He indicates the* SECOND ACTRESS *with a vague gesture.*] To me *she* [*The* MOTHER] is Amalia. But suit yourself . . . [*He is getting more and more confused.*] I don't know what to tell you . . . I'm beginning to . . . oh, I don't know . . . to find my own words ringing false, they sound different somehow.

DIRECTOR. Don't bother about that, just don't bother about it. We can always find the right sound. As for the name, if you say Amalia, Amalia it shall be; or we'll find another. For now, we'll designate the characters thus: [*To the* JUVENILE LEAD] You're the Son. [*To the* LEADING LADY] You, ma'am, are of course the Stepdaughter.

STEPDAUGHTER [*excitedly*]. What, what? That one there is me? [*She bursts out laughing.*]

DIRECTOR [*mad*]. What is there to laugh at?

LEADING LADY [*aroused*]. No one has ever dared laugh at me! I insist on respect—or I quit!

STEPDAUGHTER. But, excuse me, I'm not laughing at you.

DIRECTOR [*to the* STEPDAUGHTER]. You should consider yourself honored to be played by . . .

LEADING LADY [*without pause, contemptuously*].—"That one there!"

STEPDAUGHTER. But I wasn't speaking of you, believe me. I was speaking of me. I don't see me in you, that's all. I don't know why . . . I guess you're just not like me!

FATHER. That's it, exactly, my dear sir! What is *expressed* in us . . .

DIRECTOR. Expression, expression! You think that's your business? Not at all!

FATHER. Well, but what *we* express . . .

DIRECTOR. But you don't. You don't express. You provide us with raw material. The actors give it body and face, voice and gesture. They've given expression to much loftier material, let me tell you. Yours is on such a small scale that, if it stands up on stage at all, the credit, believe me, should all go to my actors.

FATHER. I don't dare contradict you, sir, but it's terribly painful for us who are as you see us—with these bodies, these faces—

DIRECTOR [*cutting in, out of patience*].—that's where make-up comes in, my dear sir, for whatever concerns the face, the remedy is make-up!

FATHER. Yes. But the voice, gesture—

DIRECTOR. Oh, for Heaven's sake! You can't exist here! Here the actor acts you, and that's that!

FATHER. I understand, sir. But now perhaps I begin to guess also why our author who saw us, alive as we

are, did not want to put us on stage. I don't want to
offend your actors. God forbid! But I feel that seeing
myself acted . . . I don't know by whom . . .

LEADING MAN [*rising with dignity and coming over, followed by the gay young Actresses who laugh*]. By me, if
you've no objection.

FATHER [*humble, smooth*]. I'm very honored, sir. [*He
bows.*] But however much art and willpower the
gentleman puts into absorbing me into himself . . .
[*He is bewildered now.*]

LEADING MAN. Finish. Finish.

[*The Actresses laugh.*]

FATHER. Well, the performance he will give, even forcing himself with make-up to resemble me, well,
with that figure [*all the Actors laugh*] he can hardly
play me as I am. I shall rather be—even apart from
the face—what he interprets me to be, as he feels I
am—if he feels I am anything—and not as I feel myself inside myself. And it seems to me that whoever
is called upon to judge us should take this into
account.

DIRECTOR. So now you're thinking of what the critics
will say? And I was still listening! Let the critics say
what they want. We will concentrate on putting on
your play! [*He walks away a little, and looks around.*]
Come on, come on. Is the set ready? [*To the Actors
and the Characters*] Don't clutter up the stage, I want
to be able to see! [*He goes down from the stage.*] Let's
not lose any more time! [*To the* STEPDAUGHTER] Does
the set seem pretty good to you?

STEPDAUGHTER. Oh! But I can't recognize it!

DIRECTOR. Oh my God, don't tell me we should recon-
struct Madam Pace's back room for you! [*To the
FATHER*] Didn't you say a parlor with flowered
wallpaper?

FATHER. Yes, sir. White.

DIRECTOR. It's not white. Stripes. But it doesn't matter. As for furniture we're in pretty good shape. That little table—bring it forward a bit! [*Stagehands do this. To the* PROPERTY MAN] Meanwhile you get an envelope, possibly a light blue one, and give it to the gentleman. [*Indicating the* FATHER]

PROPERTY MAN. A letter envelope?

DIRECTOR AND FATHER. Yes, a letter envelope.

PROPERTY MAN. I'll be right back. [*He exits.*]

DIRECTOR. Come on, come on. It's the young lady's scene first. [*The* LEADING LADY *comes forward.*] No, no, wait. I said the young lady. [*Indicating the* STEPDAUGHTER] You will just watch—

STEPDAUGHTER [*adding, without pause*].—watch me live it!

LEADING LADY [*resenting this*]. I'll know how to live it too, don't worry, once I put myself in the role!

DIRECTOR [*raising his hands to his head*]. Please! No more chatter! Now, scene one. The Young Lady with Madam Pace. Oh, and how about this Madam Pace? [*Bewildered, looking around him, he climbs back on stage.*]

FATHER. She isn't with us, sir.

DIRECTOR. Then what do we do?

FATHER. But she's alive. She's alive too.

DIRECTOR. Fine. But where?

FATHER. I'll tell you. [*Turning to the Actresses*] If you ladies will do me the favor of giving me your hats for a moment.

THE ACTRESSES [*surprised a little, laughing a little, in chorus*].—What?—Our hats?—What does he say?—Why?—Oh, dear!

DIRECTOR. What are you going to do with the ladies' hats?

[*The Actors laugh.*]

FATHER. Oh, nothing. Just put them on these coathooks for a minute. And would some of you be so kind as to take your coats off too?

ACTORS [*as before*]. Their coats too?—And then?— He's nuts!

AN ACTRESS OR TWO [*as above*].—But why?—Just the coats?

FATHER. Just so they can be hung there for a moment. Do me this favor. Will you?

ACTRESSES [*taking their hats off, and one or two of them their coats, too, continuing to laugh, and going to hang the hats here and there on the coathooks*].—Well, why not?—There!—This is getting to be really funny!— Are we to put them on display?

FATHER. Exactly! That's just right, ma'am: on display!

DIRECTOR. May one inquire *why* you are doing this?

FATHER. Yes, sir. If we set the stage better, who knows but she may come to us, drawn by the objects of her trade . . . [*Inviting them to look toward the entrance at the back*] Look! Look!

[*The entrance at the back opens, and* MADAM PACE *walks a few paces downstage, a hag of enormous fatness with a pompous wig of carrot-colored wool and a fiery red rose on one side of it,* à l'espagnole, *heavily made up, dressed with gauche elegance in garish red silk, a feathered fan in one hand and the other hand raised to hold a lighted cigarette between two fingers. At the sight of this apparition, the* DIRECTOR *and the Actors at once dash off the stage with a yell of terror, rushing down the stairs and making as if to flee up the aisle. The* STEPDAUGHTER, *on the other hand, runs to* MADAM PACE—*deferentially, as to her boss.*]

STEPDAUGHTER [*running to her*]. Here she is, here she is!

FATHER [*beaming*]. It's she! What did I tell you? Here she is!

DIRECTOR [*overcoming his first astonishment, and incensed now*]. What tricks are these?

[*The next four speeches are more or less simultaneous.*]

LEADING MAN. What goes on around here?
JUVENILE LEAD. Where on earth did she come from?
INGENUE. They must have been holding her in reserve.
LEADING LADY. Hocus pocus! Hocus pocus!
FATHER [*dominating these protests*]. Excuse me, though! Why, actually, would you want to destroy this prodigy in the name of vulgar truth, this miracle of a reality that is born of the stage itself—called into being by the stage, drawn here by the stage, and shaped by the stage—and which has more right to live on the stage than you have because it is much truer? Which of you actresses will later re-create Madam Pace? This lady *is* Madam Pace. You must admit that the actress who re-creates her will be less true than this lady—who is Madam Pace. Look: my daughter recognized her, and went over to her. Stand and watch the scene!

[*Hesitantly, the* DIRECTOR *and the Actors climb back on stage. But the scene between the* STEPDAUGHTER *and* MADAM PACE *has begun during the protest of the Actors and the* FATHER's *answer: sotto voce, very quietly, in short naturally—as would never be possible on a stage. When, called to order by the* FATHER, *the Actors turn again to watch, they hear* MADAM PACE, *who has just placed her hand under the* STEPDAUGHTER's *chin in order to raise her head, talk unintelligibly. After trying to hear for a moment, they just give up.*]

DIRECTOR. Well?
LEADING MAN. What's she saying?
LEADING LADY. One can't hear a thing.

JUVENILE LEAD. Louder!

STEPDAUGHTER [*leaving* MADAM PACE, *who smiles a price-less smile, and walking toward the Actors*]. Louder, huh? How d'you mean: louder? These aren't things that can be said louder. *I* was able to say them loudly—to shame him [*indicating the* FATHER]—that was my revenge. For Madam, it's different, my friends: it would mean—jail.

DIRECTOR. Oh my God! It's like that, is it? But, my dear young lady, in the theater one must be heard. And even we couldn't hear you, right here on the stage. How about an audience out front? There's a scene to be done. And anyway you *can* speak loudly—it's just between yourselves, we won't be standing here listening like now. Pretend you're alone. In a room. The back room of the shop. No one can hear you. [*The* STEPDAUGHTER *charmingly and with a mischievous smile tells him No with a repeated movement of the finger.*] Why not?

STEPDAUGHTER [*sotto voce, mysteriously*]. There's some-one who'll hear if she [MADAM PACE] speaks loudly.

DIRECTOR [*in consternation*]. Is someone else going to pop up now?

[*The Actors make as if to quit the stage again.*]

FATHER. No, no, sir. She means me. I'm to be there—behind the door—waiting. And Madam knows. So if you'll excuse me. I must be ready for my entrance. [*He starts to move.*]

DIRECTOR [*stopping him*]. No, wait. We must respect the exigencies of the theater. Before you get ready—

STEPDAUGHTER [*interrupting him*]. Let's get on with it! I tell you I'm dying with desire to live it, to live that scene! If he's ready, I'm more than ready!

DIRECTOR [*shouting*]. But first we have to get that scene

out of you and her! [*Indicating* MADAM PACE] Do you
follow me?

STEPDAUGHTER. Oh dear, oh dear, she was telling me
things you already know—that my mother's work
had been badly done once again, the material is ruined, and I'm going to have to bear with her if I
want her to go on helping us in our misery.

MADAM PACE [*coming forward with a great air of importance*]. Si, si, senor, porque yo no want profit. No advantage, no.

DIRECTOR [*almost scared*]. What, what? She talks like
that?!

[*All the Actors loudly burst out laughing.*]

STEPDAUGHTER [*also laughing*]. Yes, sir, she talks like
that—halfway between Spanish and English—very
funny, isn't it?

MADAM PACE. Now that is not good manners, no, that
you laugh at me! Yo hablo the English as good I can,
senor!

DIRECTOR. And it *is* good! Yes! Do talk that way,
ma'am! It's a sure-fire effect! There couldn't be
anything better to, um, soften the crudity of the
situation! Do talk that way! It's fine!

STEPDAUGHTER. Fine! Of course! To have certain propo-
sitions put to you in a lingo like that. Sure fire, isn't
it? Because, sir, it seems almost a joke. When I
hear there's "an old senor" who wants to "have
good time conmigo," I start to laugh—don't I,
Madam Pace?

MADAM PACE. Old, viejo, no. Viejito—leetle beet old, si,
darling? Better like that: if he no give you fun, he
bring you prudencia.

MOTHER [*jumping up, to the stupefaction and consternation of all the Actors, who had been taking no notice of
her, and who now respond to her shouts with a start and,*

smiling, try to restrain her, because she has grabbed MADAM PACE's *wig and thrown it on the floor*]. Witch! Witch! Murderess! My daughter!

STEPDAUGHTER [*running over to·restrain her* MOTHER]. No, no, mama, no, please!

FATHER [*running over too at the same time*]. Calm down, calm down! Sit here.

MOTHER. Then send that woman away!

STEPDAUGHTER [*to the* DIRECTOR, *who also has run over*]. It's not possible, not possible that my mother should be here!

FATHER [*also to the* DIRECTOR.] They can't be together. That's why, you see, the woman wasn't with us when we came. Their being together would spoil it, you understand.

DIRECTOR. It doesn't matter, doesn't matter at all. This is just a preliminary sketch. Everything helps. However confusing the elements, I'll piece them together somehow. [*Turning to the* MOTHER *and sitting her down again in her place*] Come along, come along, ma'am, calm down: sit down again.

STEPDAUGHTER [*who meanwhile has moved center stage again. Turning to* MADAM PACE]. All right, let's go!

MADAM PACE. Ah, no! No thank you! Yo aqui no do nada with your mother present.

STEPDAUGHTER. Oh, come on! Bring in that old senor who wants to have good time conmigo! [*Turning imperiously to all the others*] Yes, we've got to have it, this scene!—Come on, let's go! [*To* MADAM PACE] You may leave.

MADAM PACE. Ah si, I go, I go, go seguramente . . . [*She makes her exit furiously, putting her wig back on, and looking haughtily at the Actors who applaud mockingly.*]

STEPDAUGHTER [*to the* FATHER]. And you can make your entrance. No need to go out and come in again. Come here. Pretend, you're already in. Right. Now I'm here with bowed head, modest, huh? Let's go!

Speak up! With a different voice, the voice of someone just in off the street: "Hello, miss."
DIRECTOR [*by this time out front again*]. No look: are you
directing this, or am I? [*To the* FATHER *who looks unde-
cided and perplexed.*] Do it, yes. Go to the back. Don't
leave the stage, though. And then come forward.

[*The* FATHER *does it, almost dismayed. Very pale; but already clothed in the reality of his created life, he smiles as he
approaches from the back, as if still alien to the drama which
will break upon him. The Actors now pay attention to the
scene which is beginning.*]

DIRECTOR [*softly, in haste, to the* PROMPTER *in the box*].
And you, be ready now, ready to write!

THE SCENE

FATHER [*coming forward, with a different voice*]. Hello, miss.

STEPDAUGHTER [*with bowed head and contained disgust*]. Hello.

FATHER [*scrutinizing her under her hat which almost hides her face and noting that she is very young, exclaims, almost to himself, a little out of complaisance and a little out of fear of compromising himself in a risky adventure*]. Oh ... —Well, I was thinking, it wouldn't be the first time, hm? The first time you came here.

STEPDAUGHTER [*as above*]. No, sir.

FATHER. You've been here other times? [*And when the* STEPDAUGHTER *nods*] More than one? [*He waits a moment for her to answer, then again scrutinizes her under her hat; smiles; then says*] Well then, hm ... it shouldn't any longer be so ... May I take this hat off for you?

STEPDAUGHTER [*without pause, to forestall him, not now containing her disgust*]. No, sir, I will take it off! [*And she does so in haste, convulsed.*]

[*The* MOTHER, *watching the scene with the* SON *and with the two others, smaller and more her own, who are close to her all the time, forming a group at the opposite side of the stage from the Actors, is on tenterhooks as she follows the words and actions of* FATHER *and* STEPDAUGHTER *with varied expression: grief, disdain, anxiety, horror, now hiding her face, now emitting a moan.*]

MOTHER. Oh God! My God!

FATHER [*is momentarily turned to stone by the moaning;*

then he reassumes the previous tone]. Now give it to me: I'll hang it up for you. [*He takes the hat from her hands.*] But I could wish for a little hat worthier of such a dear, lovely little head! Would you like to help me choose one? From the many Madam has?— You wouldn't?

INGENUE [*interrupting*]. Oh now, come on, those are *our* hats!

DIRECTOR [*without pause, very angry*]. Silence, for Heaven's sake, don't try to be funny!—This is the stage. [*Turning back to the* STEPDAUGHTER] Would you begin again, please?

STEPDAUGHTER [*beginning again*]. No, thank you, sir.

FATHER. Oh, come on now, don't say no. Accept one from me. To please me ... There are some lovely ones you know. And we would make Madam happy. Why else does she put them on display?

STEPDAUGHTER. No, no, sir, look: I wouldn't even be able to wear it.

FATHER. You mean because of what the family would think when they saw you come home with a new hat on? Think nothing of it. Know how to handle that? What to tell them at home?

STEPDAUGHTER [*breaking out, at the end of her rope*]. But that's not why, sir. I couldn't wear it because I'm ... as you see me. You might surely have noticed! [*Points to her black attire.*]

FATHER. In mourning, yes. Excuse me. It's true: I do see it. I beg your pardon. I'm absolutely mortified, believe me.

STEPDAUGHTER [*forcing herself and plucking up courage to conquer her contempt and nausea*]. Enough! Enough! It's for me to thank you, it is not for you to be mortified or afflicted. Please pay no more attention to what I said. Even for me, you understand ... [*She forces herself to smile and adds*] I need to forget I am dressed like this.

DIRECTOR [*interrupting, addressing himself to the* PROMPTER *in his box, and going up on stage again*]. Wait! Wait! Don't write. Leave that last sentence out, leave it out! [*Turning to the* FATHER *and* STEPDAUGHTER] It's going very well indeed. [*Then to the* FATHER *alone*] This is where you go into the part we prepared. [*To the Actors*] Enchanting, that little hat scene, don't you agree?

STEPDAUGHTER. Oh, but the best is just coming. Why aren't we continuing?

DIRECTOR. Patience one moment. [*Again addressing himself to the Actors*] Needs rather delicate handling, of course . . .

LEADING MAN. —With a certain *ease*—

LEADING LADY. Obviously. But there's nothing to it. [*To the* LEADING MAN] We can rehearse it at once, can't we?

LEADING MAN. As far as I'm . . . Very well, I'll go out and make my entrance. [*And he does go out by the back door, ready to re-enter.*]

DIRECTOR [*to the* LEADING LADY]. And so, look, your scene with that Madam Pace is over. I'll write it up later. You are standing . . . Hey, where are you going?

LEADING LADY. Wait. I'm putting my hat back on . . . [*She does so, taking the hat from the hook.*]

DIRECTOR. Oh yes, good.—Now, you're standing here with your head bowed.

STEPDAUGHTER [*amused*]. But she's not wearing black!

LEADING LADY. I *shall* wear black! And I'll carry it better than you!

DIRECTOR [*to the* STEPDAUGHTER]. Keep quiet, please! Just watch. You can learn something. [*Claps his hands*] Get going, get going! The entrance! [*And he goes back out front to get an impression of the stage.*]

[*The door at the back opens, and the* LEADING MAN *comes forward, with the relaxed, waggish manner of an elderly Don Juan. From the first speeches, the performance of the scene by the Actors is quite a different thing, without, however, having any element of parody in it—rather, it seems corrected, set to rights. Naturally, the* STEPDAUGHTER *and the* FATHER, *being quite unable to recognize themselves in this* LEADING LADY *and* LEADING MAN *but hearing them speak their own words, express in various ways, now with gestures, now with smiles, now with open protests, their surprise, their wonderment, their suffering, etc., as will be seen forthwith.*

The PROMPTER's *voice is clearly heard from the box.*[6]]

LEADING MAN. Hello, miss.
FATHER [*without pause, unable to contain himself*]. No, no!

[*The* STEPDAUGHTER, *seeing how the* LEADING MAN *makes his entrance, has burst out laughing.*]

DIRECTOR [*coming from the proscenium, furious*]. Silence here! And stop that laughing at once! We can't go ahead till it stops.
STEPDAUGHTER [*coming from the proscenium*]. How can I help it? This lady [*the* LEADING LADY] just stands there. If she's supposed to be me, let me tell you that if anyone said hello to me in that manner and that tone of voice, I'd burst out laughing just as I actually did!
FATHER [*coming forward a little too*]. That's right . . . the manner, the tone . . .
DIRECTOR. Manner! Tone! Stand to one side now, and let me see the rehearsal.
LEADING MAN [*coming forward*]. If I'm to play an old man entering a house of ill—
DIRECTOR. Oh, pay no attention, please. Just begin again. It was going fine. [*Waiting for the Actor to resume*] Now then . . .

LEADING MAN. Hello, miss.

LEADING LADY. Hello.

LEADING MAN [*re-creating the* FATHER'S *gesture of scrutinizing her under her hat, but then expressing very distinctly first the complaisance and then the fear*]. Oh . . . Well . . . I was thinking it wouldn't be the first time, I hope . . .

FATHER [*unable to help correcting him*]. Not "I hope." "Would it?" "Would it?"

DIRECTOR. He says: "would it?" A question.

LEADING MAN [*pointing to the* PROMPTER]. I heard: "I hope."

DIRECTOR. Same thing! "Would it." Or: "I hope." Continue, continue.—Now, maybe a bit less affected . . . Look, I'll do it for you. Watch me . . . [*Returns to the stage, then repeats the bit since the entrance*]— Hello, miss.

LEADING LADY. Hello.

DIRECTOR. Oh, well . . . I was thinking . . . [*Turning to the* LEADING MAN *to have him note how he has looked at the* LEADING LADY *under her hat*] Surprise . . . fear and complaisance. [*Then, going on, and turning to the* LEADING LADY] It wouldn't be the first time, would it? The first time you came here. [*Again turning to the* LEADING MAN *with an inquiring look*] Clear? [*To the* LEADING LADY] Then you say: No, sir [*Back to the* LEADING MAN] How shall I put it? Plasticity! [*Goes back out front.*]

LEADING LADY. No, sir.

LEADING MAN. You came here other times? More than one?

DIRECTOR. No, no, wait. [*Indicating the* LEADING LADY] First let her nod. "You came here other times?"

[*The* LEADING LADY *raises her head a little, closes her eyes painfully as if in disgust, then nods it twice at the word "Down" from the* DIRECTOR.]

STEPDAUGHTER [*involuntarily*]. Oh, my God! [*And she at once puts her hand on her mouth to keep the laughter in.*]

DIRECTOR [*turning round*]. What is it?

STEPDAUGHTER [*without pause*]. Nothing, nothing.

DIRECTOR [*to the* LEADING MAN]. That's your cue. Go straight on.

LEADING MAN. More than one? Well then, hm ... it shouldn't any longer be so ... May I take this little hat off for you?

[*The* LEADING MAN *says this last speech in such a tone and accompanies it with such a gesture that the* STEP-DAUGHTER, *her hands on her mouth, much as she wants to hold herself in, cannot contain her laughter, which comes bursting out through her fingers irresistibly and very loud.*]

LEADING LADY [*returning to her place, enraged*]. Now look, I'm not going to be made a clown of by that person!

LEADING MAN. Nor am I. Let's stop.

DIRECTOR [*to the* STEPDAUGHTER, *roaring*]. Stop it! Stop it!

STEPDAUGHTER. Yes, yes. Forgive me, forgive me ...

DIRECTOR. You have no manners! You're presumptuous! So there!

FATHER [*seeking to intervene*]. That's true, yes, that's true, sir, but forgive ...

DIRECTOR [*on stage again*]. Forgive nothing! It's disgusting!

FATHER. Yes, sir. But believe me, it has such a strange effect—

DIRECTOR. Strange? Strange? What's strange about it?

FATHER. I admire your actors, sir, I really admire them, this gentleman [LEADING MAN] and that lady [LEAD-ING LADY] but assuredly ... well, they're not us ...

DIRECTOR. So what? How *could* they be you, if they're the actors?

FATHER. Exactly, the actors! And they play our parts well, both of them. But of course, to us, they seem something else—that tries to be the same but simply isn't!

DIRECTOR. How d'you mean: isn't? What is it then?

FATHER. Something that . . . becomes theirs. And stops being ours.

DIRECTOR. Necessarily! I explained that to you!

FATHER. Yes. I understand, I do under—

DIRECTOR. Then that will be enough! [*Turning to the Actors.*] We'll be rehearsing by ourselves as we usually do. Rehearsing with authors present has always been hell, in my experience. There's no satisfying them. [*Turning to the* FATHER *and the* STEPDAUGHTER] Come along then. Let's resume. And let's hope you find it possible not to laugh this time.

STEPDAUGHTER. Oh, no, I won't be laughing this time around. My big moment comes up now. Don't worry!

DIRECTOR. Very well, when she says: "Please pay no more attention to what I said . . . Even for me—you understand . . ." [*Turning to the* FATHER] You'll have to cut right in with: "I understand, oh yes, I understand . . ." and ask her right away—

STEPDAUGHTER [*interrupting*]. Oh? Ask me what?

DIRECTOR. —why she is in mourning.

STEPDAUGHTER. No, no, look: when I told him I needed to forget I was dressed like this, do you know what his answer was? "Oh, good! Then let's take that little dress right off, shall we?"

DIRECTOR. Great! Terrific! It'll knock 'em right out of their seats!

STEPDAUGHTER. But it's the truth.

DIRECTOR. Truth, is it? Well, well, well. This is the theater! Our motto is: truth up to a certain point!

STEPDAUGHTER. Then what would you propose?

DIRECTOR. You'll see. You'll see it. Just leave me alone.

STEPDAUGHTER. Certainly not. From my nausea—from all the reasons one more cruel than another why I am what I am, why I am "that one there"—you'd like to cook up some romantic, sentimental concoction, wouldn't you? He asks me why I'm in mourning, and I tell him, through my tears, that Papa died two months ago! No, my dear sir! He has to say what he did say: "Then let's take that little dress right off, shall we?" And I, with my two-months mourning in my heart, went back there—you see? behind that screen—and—my fingers quivering with shame, with loathing—I took off my dress, took off my corset . . .

DIRECTOR [*running his hands through his hair*]. Good God, what are you saying?

STEPDAUGHTER [*shouting frantically*]. The truth, sir, the truth!

DIRECTOR. Well, yes, of course, that must be the truth . . . and I quite understand your horror, young lady. Would you try to understand that all that is impossible *on the stage*?

STEPDAUGHTER. Impossible? Then, thanks very much, I'm leaving.

DIRECTOR. No, no, look . . .

STEPDAUGHTER. I'm leaving, I'm leaving! You went in that room, you two, didn't you, and figured out "what is possible on the stage"? Thanks very much. I see it all. He wants to skip to the point where he can act out his [*exaggerating*] spiritual travail! But I want to play *my* drama. Mine!

DIRECTOR [*annoyed, and shrugging haughtily*]. Oh, well, *your* drama. This is not just your drama, if I may say so. How about the drama of the others? His drama [*the* FATHER], hers [*the* MOTHER]? We can't let one character hog the limelight, just taking the whole stage over, and overshadowing all the others! Everything must be placed within the frame of one harmonious picture! We must perform only what is performable! I know as well as you do that each of us has a whole life of his own inside him and would like to bring it all out. But the difficult thing is this: to bring out only as much as is needed—in relation to the others—and in this to *imply* all the rest, *suggest* what remains inside! Oh, it would be nice if every character could come down to the footlights and tell the audience just what is brewing inside him—in a fine monologue or, if you will, a lecture! [*Good-natured, conciliatory*] Miss, you will have to *contain yourself*. And it will be in your interest. It could make a bad impression—let me warn you— this tearing fury, this desperate disgust—since, if I may say so, you confessed having been with others at Madam Pace's—before him—more than once!

STEPDAUGHTER [*lowering her head, pausing to recollect, a deeper note in her voice*]. It's true. But to me the others are also *him*, all of them equally!

DIRECTOR [*not getting it*]. The others? How d'you mean?

STEPDAUGHTER. People "go wrong." And wrong follows on the heels of wrong. Who is responsible, if not whoever it was who first brought them down? Isn't that always the case? And for me that is him. Even before I was born. Look at him, and see if it isn't so.

DIRECTOR. Very good. And if he has so much to feel guilty about, can't you appreciate how it must weigh him down? So let's at least permit him to act it out.

STEPDAUGHTER. And how, may I ask, how could he act out all that "noble" guilt, all those so "moral" torments, if you propose to spare him the horror of one day finding in his arms—after having bade her take off the black clothes that marked her recent loss—a woman now, and already gone wrong—that little girl, sir, that little girl whom he used to go watch coming out of school?

[*She says these last words in a voice trembling with emotion. The* MOTHER, *hearing her say this, overcome with uncontrollable anguish, which comes out first in suffocated moans and subsequently bursts out in bitter weeping. The emotion takes hold of everyone. Long pause.*]

STEPDAUGHTER [*as soon as the* MOTHER *gives signs of calming down, somber, determined*]. We're just among ourselves now. Still unknown to the public. Tomorrow you will make of us the show you have in mind. You will put it together in your way. But would you like to really see—our drama? Have it explode—the real thing?

DIRECTOR. Of course. Nothing I'd like better. And I'll use as much of it as I possibly can!

STEPDAUGHTER. Very well. Have this Mother here go out.

MOTHER [*ceasing to weep, with a loud cry*]. No, no! Don't allow this, don't allow it!

DIRECTOR. I only want to take a look, ma'am.

MOTHER. I can't, I just can't!

DIRECTOR. But if it's already happened? Excuse me but I just don't get it.

MOTHER. No, no, it's happening now. It's always happening. My torment is not a pretense! I am alive and present—always, in every moment of my torment—it keeps renewing itself, it too is alive and always present. But those two little ones over there—have you heard them speak? They cannot speak, sir, not any more! They still keep clinging to me—to keep my torment alive and present. For themselves they don't exist, don't exist any longer. And she [*the* STEPDAUGHTER], she just fled, ran away from me, she's lost, lost . . . If I see her before me now, it's for the same reason: to renew the torment, keep it always

alive and present forever—the torment I've suffered
on her account too—forever!

FATHER [*solemn*]. The eternal moment, sir, as I told you.
She [*the* STEPDAUGHTER] is here to catch me, fix
me, hold me there in the pillory, hanging there forever, hooked, in that single fleeting shameful moment of my life! She cannot give it up. And, actually,
sir, *you* cannot spare me.

DIRECTOR. But I didn't say I wouldn't use that. On the
contrary, it will be the nucleus of the whole first act.
To the point where she [*the* MOTHER] surprises you.

FATHER. Yes, exactly. Because that is the sentence
passed upon me: all our passion which has to culmi-
nate in her [*the* MOTHER's] final cry!

STEPDAUGHTER. It still rings in my ears. It's driven me
out of my mind, that cry!—You can present me as
you wish, sir, it doesn't matter. Even dressed. As
long as at least my arms—just my arms—are bare.
Because it was like this. [*She goes to the* FATHER *and
rests her head on his chest.*] I was standing like this
with my head on his chest and my arms round his
neck like this. Then I saw something throbbing right
here on my arm. A vein. Then, as if it was just this
living vein that disgusted me, I jammed my eyes
shut, like this, d'you see? and buried my head on his
chest. [*Turning to the* MOTHER] Scream, scream,
mama! [*Buries her head on the* FATHER's *chest and with
her shoulders raised as if to avoid hearing the scream she
adds in a voice stifled with torment.*] Scream as you
screamed then!

MOTHER [*rushing forward to part them*]. No! My daughter!
My daughter! [*Having pulled her from him*] Brute! Brute!
It's my daughter, don't you see—my daughter!

DIRECTOR [*the outburst having sent him reeling to the footlights, while the Actors show dismay*]. Fine! Splendid!
And now: curtain, curtain!

FATHER [*running to him, convulsed*]. Right! Yes! Because
that, sir, is how it actually was!

DIRECTOR [*in admiration and conviction*]. Yes, yes, of
course! Curtain! Curtain!

[*Hearing this repeated cry of the* DIRECTOR, *the* TECHNI-
CIAN *lets down the curtain, trapping the* DIRECTOR *and the*
FATHER *between curtain and footlights.*]

DIRECTOR [*looking up, with raised arms*]. What an idiot! I
say Curtain, meaning that's how the act should end,
and they let down the actual curtain! [*He lifts a corner of the curtain so he can get back on stage. To the* FA-
THER] Yes, yes, fine, splendid! Absolutely sure fire!
Has to end that way. I can vouch for the first act.
[*Goes behind the curtain with the* FATHER.]

[*When the curtain rises we see that the stagehands have
struck that first "indication of a set," and have put on stage
in its stead a small garden fountain. On one side of the
stage, the Actors are sitting in a row, and on the other are
the Characters. The* DIRECTOR *is standing in the middle of
the stage, in the act of meditating with one hand, fist
clenched, on his mouth.*]

DIRECTOR [*shrugging after a short pause*]. Yes, well then,
let's get to the second act. Just leave it to me as we
agreed beforehand and everything will be all right.

STEPDAUGHTER. Our entrance into his house [*the* FA-
THER] in spite of him. [*the* SON]

DIRECTOR [*losing patience*]. Very well. But leave it all to
me, I say.

STEPDAUGHTER. In spite of him. Just let that be clear.

MOTHER [*shaking her head from her corner*]. For all the
good that's come out of it . . .

STEPDAUGHTER [*turning quickly on her*]. It doesn't

matter. The more damage to us, the more guilt feelings for him.

DIRECTOR [*still out of patience*]. I understand, I understand. All this will be taken into account, especially at the beginning. Rest assured.

MOTHER [*supplicatingly*]. Do make them understand, I beg you, sir, for my conscience sake, for I tried in every possible way—

STEPDAUGHTER [*continuing her* MOTHER's *speech, contemptuously*]. To placate me, to advise me not to give him trouble. [*To the* DIRECTOR] Do what she wants, do it because it's true. I enjoy the whole thing very much because, look: the more she plays the suppliant and tries to gain entrance into his heart, the more he holds himself aloof: he's an absentee! How I relish this!

DIRECTOR. We want to get going—on the second act, don't we?

STEPDAUGHTER. I won't say another word. But to play it all in the garden, as you want to, won't be possible.

DIRECTOR. Why won't it be possible?

STEPDAUGHTER. Because he [*the* SON] stays shut up in his room, on his own. Then again we need the house for the part about this poor bewildered little boy, as I told you.

DIRECTOR. Quite right. But on the other hand, we can't change the scenery in view of the audience three or four times in one act, nor can we stick up signs—

LEADING MAN. They used to at one time . . .

DIRECTOR. Yes, when the audiences were about as mature as that little girl.

LEADING LADY. They got the illusion more easily.

FATHER [*suddenly, rising*]. The illusion, please don't say illusion! Don't use that word! It's especially cruel to us.

DIRECTOR [*astonished*]. And why, if I may ask?

FATHER. Oh yes, cruel, cruel! You should understand that.

DIRECTOR. What word would you have us use anyway? The illusion of creating here for our spectators—

LEADING MAN. —By our performance—

DIRECTOR. —the illusion of a reality.

FATHER. I understand, sir, but perhaps you do not understand us. Because, you see, for you and for your actors all this—quite rightly—is a game—

LEADING LADY [*indignantly interrupting*]. Game! We are not children, sir. We act in earnest.

FATHER. I don't deny it. I just mean the game of your art which, as this gentleman rightly says, must provide a perfect illusion of reality.

DIRECTOR. Yes, exactly.

FATHER. But consider this. We [*he quickly indicates himself and the other five Characters*], we have no reality outside this illusion.

DIRECTOR [*astonished, looking at his Actors who remain bewildered and lost*]. And that means?

FATHER [*after observing them briefly, with a pale smile*]. Just that, ladies and gentlemen. How should we have any other reality? What for you is an illusion, to be created, is for us our unique reality. [*Short pause. He takes several short steps toward the DIRECTOR, and adds*] But not for us alone, of course. Think a moment. [*He looks into his eyes.*] Can you tell me who you are? [*And he stands there pointing his first finger at him.*]

DIRECTOR [*Upset, with a half-smile*]. How do you mean, who I am? I am I.

FATHER. And if I told you that wasn't true because you are me?

DIRECTOR. I would reply that you are out of your mind. [*The Actors laugh.*]

FATHER. You are right to laugh: because this is a game.

[*To the* DIRECTOR] And you can object that it's only in a game that that gentleman there [LEADING MAN], who is himself, must be me, who am *my*self. I've caught you in a trap, do you see that?

[*Actors start laughing again.*]

DIRECTOR [*annoyed*]. You said all this before. Why repeat it?

FATHER. I won't—I didn't intend to say that. I'm inviting you to emerge from this game. [*He looks at the* LEADING LADY *as if to forestall what she might say.*] This game of art which you are accustomed to play here with your actors. Let me again ask quite seriously: Who are you?

DIRECTOR [*turning to the Actors, amazed and at the same time irritated*]. The gall of this fellow! Calls himself a character and comes here to ask me who I am!

FATHER [*dignified, but not haughty*]. A character, sir, can always ask a man who he is. Because a character really has his own life, marked with his own characteristics, by virtue of which he is always someone. Whereas, a man—I'm not speaking of you now—*a man* can be no one.

DIRECTOR. Oh sure. But you are asking me! And I am the manager, understand?

FATHER [*quite softly with mellifluous modesty*]. Only in order to know, sir, if you as you now are see yourself ... for example, at a distance in time. Do you see the man you once were, with all the illusions you had then, with everything, inside you and outside, as it seemed then—as it was then for you!— Well sir, thinking back to those illusions which you don't have any more, to all those things which no longer seem to be what at one time they were for you, don't you feel, not just the boards of this stage, but the very earth beneath slipping away from you?

For will not all that you feel yourself to be now, your whole reality of today, as it is now, inevitably seem an illusion tomorrow?

DIRECTOR [*who has not followed exactly, but has been staggered by the plausibilities of the argument*]. Well, well, what do you want to prove?

FATHER. Oh nothing sir. I just wanted to make you see that if *we* [*pointing again at himself and the other Characters*] have no reality outside of illusion, it would be well if you should distrust your reality because, though you breathe it and touch it today, it is destined like that of yesterday to stand revealed to you tomorrow as illusion.

DIRECTOR [*deciding to mock him*]. Oh splendid! And you'll be telling me next that you and this play that you have come to perform for me are truer and more real than I am.

FATHER [*quite seriously*]. There can be no doubt of that, sir.

DIRECTOR. Really?

FATHER. I thought you had understood that from the start.

DIRECTOR. More real than me?

FATHER. If your reality can change overnight . . .

DIRECTOR. Of course it can, it changes all the time, like everyone else's.

FATHER [*with a cry*]. But ours does not, sir. You see, that is the difference. It does not change, it cannot ever change or be otherwise because it is already fixed, it is what is, just that, forever—a terrible thing, sir!—an immutable reality. You should shudder to come near us.[7]

DIRECTOR [*suddenly struck by a new idea, he steps in front of the* FATHER]. I should like to know, however, when anyone ever saw a character get out of his part and set about expounding and explicating it, delivering lectures on it. Can you tell me? I have never seen anything like that.

FATHER. You have never seen it, sir, because authors generally hide the travail of their creations. When characters are alive and turn up, living, before their author, all that author does is follow the words and gestures which they propose to him. He has to want them to be as they themselves want to be. Woe betide him if he doesn't! When a character is born, he at once acquires such an independence, even of his own author, that the whole world can imagine him in innumerable situations other than those the author thought to place him in. At times he acquires a meaning that the author never dreamt of giving him.

DIRECTOR. Certainly, I know that.

FATHER. Then why all this astonishment at us? Imagine what a misfortune it is for a character such as I described to you—given life in the imagination of an author who then wished to deny him life—and tell me frankly: isn't such a character, given life and left without life, isn't he right to set about doing just what we are doing now as we stand here before you, after having done just the same—for a very long time, believe me—before *him*, trying to persuade him, trying to push him ... I would appear before him sometimes, sometimes she [*looks at* STEPDAUGHTER] would go to him, sometimes that poor mother ...

STEPDAUGHTER [*coming forward as if in a trance*]. It's true. I too went there, sir, to tempt him, many times, in the melancholy of that study of his, at the twilight hour, when he would sit stretched out in his armchair, unable to make up his mind to switch the light on, and letting the evening shadows invade the room, knowing that these shadows were alive with us and that we were coming to tempt him ...

[*As if she saw herself still in that study and felt only annoyance at the presence of all of these Actors*] Oh, if only you would all go away! Leave us alone! My mother there with her son—I with this little girl— the boy there always alone—then I with him [*the FA-THER*]—then I by myself, I by myself . . . in those shadows. [*Suddenly she jumps up as if she wished to take hold of herself in the vision she has of herself lighting up the shadows and alive.*] Ah my life! What scenes, what scenes we went there to propose to him: I, I tempted him more than the others.

FATHER. Right, but perhaps that was the trouble: you in-sisted too much. You thought you could seduce him.

STEPDAUGHTER. Nonsense. He wanted me that way. [*She comes up to the DIRECTOR to tell him as in confi-dence.*] If you ask me, sir, it was because he was so depressed, or because he despised the theater the public knows and wants . . .

DIRECTOR. Let's continue. Let's continue, for Heaven's sake. Enough theories, I'd like some facts. Give me some facts.

STEPDAUGHTER. It seems to me that we have already given you more facts than you can handle—with our entry into his [*the FATHER's*] house! You said you couldn't change the scene every five minutes or start hanging signs.

DIRECTOR. Nor can we, of course not, we have to com-bine the scenes and group them in one simultaneous close-knit action. Not your idea at all. You'd like to see your brother come home from school and wan-der through the house like a ghost, hiding behind the doors, and brooding on a plan which—how did you put it—?

STEPDAUGHTER. —shrivels him up, sir, completely shrivels him up, sir.

DIRECTOR. "Shrivels!" What a word! All right then: his

growth was stunted except for his eyes. Is that what you said?

STEPDAUGHTER. Yes, sir. Just look at him. [*She points him out next to the* MOTHER.]

DIRECTOR. Good girl. And then at the same time you want this little girl to be playing in the garden, dead to the world. Now, the boy in the house, the girl in the garden, is that possible?

STEPDAUGHTER. Happy in the sunshine! Yes, that is my only reward, her pleasure, her joy in that garden! After the misery, the squalor of a horrible room where we slept, all four of us, she with me: just think, of the horror of my contaminated body next to hers! She held me tight, oh so tight with her loving innocent little arms! In the garden she would run and take my hand as soon as she saw me. She did not see the big flowers, she ran around looking for the teeny ones and wanted to show them to me, oh the joy of it!

[*Saying this and tortured by the memory she breaks into prolonged desperate sobbing, dropping her head onto her arms which are spread out on the work table. Everyone is overcome by her emotion. The* DIRECTOR *goes to her almost paternally and says to comfort her*]

DIRECTOR. We'll do the garden. We'll do the garden, don't worry, and you'll be very happy about it. We'll bring all the scenes together in the garden. [*Calling a stagehand by name*] Hey, drop me a couple of trees, will you, two small cypress trees, here in front of the fountain.

[*Two small cypress trees are seen descending from the flies. A* STAGEHAND *runs on to secure them with nails and a couple of braces.*]

DIRECTOR [*to the* STEPDAUGHTER]. Something to go on with anyway. Gives us an idea. [*Again calling the* STAGEHAND *by name*] Hey, give me a bit of sky.

STAGEHAND [*from above*]. What?

DIRECTOR. Bit of sky, a backcloth, to go behind that fountain. [*A white backdrop is seen descending from the flies.*] Not white, I said sky. It doesn't matter, leave it, I'll take care of it. [*Shouting*] Hey, Electrician, put these lights out. Let's have a bit of atmosphere, lunar atmosphere, blue background, and give me a blue spot on that backcloth. That's right. That's enough. [*At his command a mysterious lunar scene is created which induces the Actors to talk and move as they would on an evening in the garden beneath the moon.*] [*To* STEPDAUGHTER] You see? And now instead of hiding behind doors in the house the boy could move around here in the garden and hide behind trees. But it will be difficult, you know, to find a little girl to play the scene where she shows you the flowers. [*Turning to the* BOY] Come down this way a bit. Let's see how this can be worked out. [*And when the* BOY *doesn't move*] Come on, come on. [*Then dragging him forward he tries to make him hold his head up but it falls down again every time.*] Oh dear, another problem, this boy ... What *is* it? ... My God, he'll have to say something ... [*He goes up to him, puts a hand on his shoulder and leads him behind one of the tree drops.*] Come on. Come on. Let me see. You can hide a bit here ... Like this ... You can stick your head out a bit to look ... [*He goes to one side to see the effect. The* BOY *has scarcely run through the actions when the Actors are deeply affected; and they remain quite overwhelmed.*] Ah! Fine! Splendid! [*He turns again to the* STEPDAUGHTER.] If the little girl surprises him looking out and runs over to him, don't you think she might drag a few words out of him too?

STEPDAUGHTER [*jumping to her feet*]. Don't expect him

to speak while *he's* here. [*She points to the* SON.] You have to send *him* away first.

SON [*going resolutely toward one of the two stairways*]. Suits me. Glad to go. Nothing I want more.

DIRECTOR [*immediately calling him*]. No. Where are you going? Wait.

[*The* MOTHER *rises, deeply moved, in anguish at the thought that he is really going. She instinctively raises her arms as if to halt him, yet without moving away from her position.*]

SON [*arriving at the footlights, where the* DIRECTOR *stops him*]. I have absolutely nothing to do here. So let me go please. Just let me go.

DIRECTOR. How do you mean, you having nothing to do?

STEPDAUGHTER [*placidly, with irony*]. Don't hold him! He won't go.

FATHER. He has to play the terrible scene in the garden with his mother.

SON [*unhesitating, resolute, proud*]. I play nothing. I said so from the start. [*To the* DIRECTOR] Let me go.

STEPDAUGHTER [*running to the* DIRECTOR *to get him to lower his arms so that he is no longer holding the* SON *back*]. Let him go. [*Then turning to the* SON *as soon as the* DIRECTOR *has let him go*] Very well, go. [*The* SON *is all set to move toward the stairs but, as if held by some occult power, he cannot go down the steps. While the Actors are both astounded and deeply troubled, he moves slowly across the footlights straight to the other stairway. But having arrived there he remains poised for the descent but unable to descend. The* STEPDAUGHTER, *who has followed him with her eyes in an attitude of defiance, bursts out laughing.*] He can't, you see. He can't. He has to stay here, has to. Bound by a chain, indissolubly. But if I who do take flight, sir, when that hap-

pens which has to happen, and precisely because of
the hatred I feel for him, precisely so as not to see
him again—very well, if *I* am still here and can bear
the sight of him and his company—you can imagine
whether *he* can go away. He who really must, must
remain here with that fine father of his and that
mother there who no longer has any other children.
[*Turning again to the* MOTHER] Come on, Mother,
come on. [*Turning again to the* DIRECTOR *and pointing
to the* MOTHER] Look, she got up to hold him back.
[*To the* MOTHER, *as if exerting a magical power over her*]
Come. Come ... [*Then to the* DIRECTOR] You can
imagine how little she wants to display her love in
front of your actors. But so great is her desire to get
at him that—look, you see—she is even prepared to
live her scene.

[*In fact the* MOTHER *has approached and no sooner has the*
STEPDAUGHTER *spoken her last words than she spreads her
arms to signify consent.*]

SON [*without pause*]. But *I* am not, *I* am not. If I can not
go I will stay here, but I repeat: I will play nothing.
FATHER [*to the* DIRECTOR, *enraged*]. You can force
him, sir.
SON. No one can force me.
FATHER. I will force you.
STEPDAUGHTER. Wait, wait. First the little girl must be
at the fountain. [*She runs to take the* LITTLE GIRL, *drops
on her knees in front of her, takes her little face in her
hands.*] My poor little darling, you look bewildered
with those lovely big eyes of yours. Who knows
where you think you are? We are on a stage my
dear. What is a stage? It is a place where you play at
being serious, a place for play-acting, where we will
now play-act. But seriously! For real! You too ...
[*She embraces her, presses her to her bosom and rocks her*

a little.] Oh, little darling, little darling, what an ugly play you will enact! What a horrible thing has been planned for you, the garden, the fountain ... All pretense, of course, that's the trouble, my sweet, everything is make-believe here, but perhaps for you, my child, a make-believe fountain is nicer than a real one for playing in, hmm? It will be a game for the others, but not for you, alas, because you are real, my darling, and are actually playing in a fountain that is real, beautiful, big, green with many bamboo plants reflected in it and giving it shade. Many, many ducklings can swim in it, breaking the shade to bits. You want to take hold of one of these ducklings ... [*With a shout that fills everyone with dismay*] No! No, my Rosetta! Your mother is not looking after you because of that beast of a son. A thousand devils are loose in my head ... and *he* ... [*She leaves the* LITTLE GIRL *and turns with her usual hostility to the* BOY.] And what are you doing here, always looking like a beggar child? It will be your fault too if this little girl drowns—with all your standing around like that. As if I hadn't paid for everybody when I got you all into this house. [*Grabbing one of his arms to force him to take a hand out of his pocket*] What have you got there? What are you hiding? Let's see this hand. [*Tears his hand out of his pocket, and to the horror of everyone discovers that it holds a small revolver. She looks at it for a moment as if satisfied and then says*] Ah! Where did you get that and how? [*And as the* BOY *in his confusion, with his eyes staring and vacant all the time, does not answer her*] Idiot, if I were you I wouldn't have killed myself, I would have killed one of those two—or both of them—the father and the son! [*She hides him behind the small cypress tree from which he had been looking out, and she takes the* LITTLE GIRL *and hides her in the fountain, having her lie down in it in such a way as to be quite* hidden. Finally, the STEPDAUGHTER *goes down on her knees with her face in her hands, which are resting on the rim of the fountain.*]

DIRECTOR. Splendid! [*Turning to the* SON] And at the same time . . .

SON [*with contempt*]. And at the same time, nothing. It is not true, sir. There was never any scene between me and her. [*He points to the* MOTHER.] Let her tell you herself how it was.

[*Meanwhile the* SECOND ACTRESS *and the* JUVENILE LEAD *have detached themselves from the group of Actors. The former has started to observe the* MOTHER, *who is opposite her, very closely. And the other has started to observe the* SON. *Both are planning how they will re-create the roles.*]

MOTHER. Yes, it is true, sir. I had gone to his room.

SON. My room, did you hear that? Not the garden.

DIRECTOR. That is of no importance. We have to re-arrange the action, I told you that.

SON [*noticing that the* JUVENILE LEAD *is observing him*]. What do *you* want?

JUVENILE LEAD. Nothing. I am observing you.

SON [*turning to the other side where the* SECOND ACTRESS *is*]. Ah, and here we have you to re-create the role, eh? [*He points to the* MOTHER.]

DIRECTOR. Exactly, exactly. You should be grateful, it seems to me, for the attention they are giving you.

SON. Oh yes, thank you. But you still haven't understood that you cannot do this drama. We are not inside you, not in the least, and your actors are looking at us from the outside. Do you think it's possible for us to live before a mirror which, not content to freeze us in the fixed image it provides of our expression, also throws back at us an unrecognizable grimace purporting to be ourselves?

FATHER. That is true. That is true. You must see that.

DIRECTOR [*to the* JUVENILE LEAD *and the* SECOND ACTRESS]. Very well, get away from here.

SON. No good. I won't cooperate.

DIRECTOR. Just be quiet a minute and let me hear your mother. [*To the* MOTHER] Well? You went into his room?

MOTHER. Yes sir, into his room. I was at the end of my tether. I wanted to pour out all of the anguish which was oppressing me. But as soon as he saw me come in—

SON. —There was no scene. I went away. I went away so there would be no scene. Because I have never made scenes, never, understand?

MOTHER. That's true. That's how it was. Yes.

DIRECTOR. But now there's got to be a scene between you and him. It is indispensable.

MOTHER. As for me, sir, I am ready. If only you could find some way to have me speak to him for one moment, to have me say what is in my heart.

FATHER [*going right up to the* SON, *very violent*]. You will do it! For your mother! For your mother!

SON [*more decisively than ever*]. I will do nothing!

FATHER [*grabbing him by the chest and shaking him*]. By God, you will obey! Can't you hear how she is talking to you? Aren't you her son?

SON [*grabbing his* FATHER]. No! No! Once and for all let's have done with it!

[*General agitation. The* MOTHER, *terrified, tries to get between them to separate them.*]

MOTHER [*as before*]. Please, please!

FATHER [*without letting go of the* SON]. You must obey, you must obey!

SON [*wrestling with his* FATHER *and in the end throwing him to the ground beside the little stairway, to the horror of everyone*]. What's this frenzy that's taken hold of you? To show your shame and ours to everyone? Have you no restraint? I won't cooperate, I won't cooperate! And that is how I interpret the wishes of the man who did not choose to put us on stage.

DIRECTOR. But you came here.

SON [*pointing to his* FATHER]. He came here—not me!

DIRECTOR. But aren't you here too?

SON. It was he who wanted to come, dragging the rest of us with him, and then getting together with you to plot not only what really happened, but also—as if that did not suffice—*what did not happen*.

DIRECTOR. Then tell me. Tell me what did happen. Just tell me. You came out of your room without saying a thing?

SON [*after a moment of hesitation*]. Without saying a thing. In order not to make a scene.

DIRECTOR [*driving him on*]. Very well, and then, what did you do then?

SON [*while everyone looks on in anguished attention, he moves a few steps on the front part of the stage*]. Nothing . . . crossing the garden . . . [*He stops, gloomy, withdrawn.*]

DIRECTOR [*always driving him on to speak, impressed by his reticence*]. Very well, crossing the garden?

SON [*desperate, hiding his face with one arm*]. Why do you want to make me say it, sir? It is horrible.

[*The* MOTHER *trembles all over, and stifles groans, looking toward the fountain.*]

DIRECTOR [*softly, noticing this look of hers, turning to the* SON, *with growing apprehension*]. The little girl?

SON [*looking out into the auditorium*]. Over there—in the fountain . . .

FATHER [*on the ground, pointing compassionately toward the* MOTHER]. And she followed him, sir.

DIRECTOR [*to the* SON, *anxiously*]. And then you . . .

SON [*slowly, looking straight ahead all the time*]. I ran out.
   I started to fish her out . . . but all of a sudden I
   stopped. Behind those trees I saw something that
   froze me: the boy, the boy was standing there, quite
   still. There was madness in the eyes. He was looking
   at his drowned sister in the fountain. [*The* STEP-
   DAUGHTER, *who has been bent over the fountain, hiding
   the* LITTLE GIRL, *is sobbing desperately, like an echo from
   the bottom. Pause*] I started to approach and then . . .

[*From behind the trees where the* BOY *has been hiding, a revolver shot rings out.*]

MOTHER [*running up with a tormented shout, accompanied
   by the* SON *and all the Actors in a general tumult*]. Son!
   My son! [*And then amid the hub-bub and the discon-
   nected shouts of the others*] Help! Help!

DIRECTOR [*amid the shouting, trying to clear a space while
   the* BOY *is lifted by his head and feet and carried away behind the backcloth*]. Is he wounded, is he wounded,
   really?

[*Everyone except the* DIRECTOR *and the* FATHER, *who has
remained on the ground beside the steps, has disappeared behind the backcloth which has served for a sky, where they
can still be heard for a while whispering anxiously. Then
from one side and the other of this curtain, the Actors come
back on stage.*]

LEADING LADY [*re-entering from the right, very much upset*]. He's dead! Poor boy! He's dead! What a terrible
   thing!

LEADING MAN [*re-entering from the left, laughing*]. How
   do you mean, dead? Fiction, fiction, one doesn't believe such things.

OTHER ACTORS [*on the right*]. Fiction? Reality! Reality!
He is dead!

OTHER ACTORS [*on the left*]. No! Fiction! Fiction!

FATHER [*rising, and crying out to them*]. Fiction indeed!
Reality, reality, gentlemen, reality! [*Desperate, he too
disappears at the back.*]

DIRECTOR [*at the end of his rope*]. Fiction! Reality! To hell
with all of you! Lights, lights, lights! [*At a single stroke
the whole stage and auditorium is flooded with very bright
light. The* DIRECTOR *breathes again, as if freed from an incubus, and they all look each other in the eyes, bewildered
and lost.*] Things like this don't happen to me, they've
made me lose a whole day. [*He looks at his watch.*]
Go, you can all go. What could we do now anyway?
It is too late to pick up the rehearsal where we left
off. See you this evening. [*As soon as the Actors have
gone he talks to the* ELECTRICIAN *by name.*] Hey, Electrician, lights out. [*He has hardly said the words when
the theater is plunged for a moment into complete dark-
ness.*] Hey, for God's sake, leave me at least one light!
I like to see where I am going!

[*Immediately, from behind the backcloth, as if the wrong
switch had been pulled, a green light comes on which pro-
jects the silhouettes, clear-cut and large, of the Characters,
minus the* BOY *and the* LITTLE GIRL. *Seeing the silhouettes,
the* DIRECTOR, *terrified, rushes from the stage. At the same
time the light behind the backcloth goes out and the stage is
again lit in nocturnal blue as before.*

Slowly, from the right side of the curtain, the SON *comes
forward first, followed by the* MOTHER *with her arms
stretched out toward him; then from the left side, the* FA-
THER. *They stop in the middle of the stage and stay there as
if in a trance. Last of all from the right, the* STEPDAUGHTER
*comes out and runs toward the two stairways. She stops
on the first step, to look for a moment at the other three,*

*and then breaks into a harsh laugh before throwing herself
down the steps; she runs down the aisle between the rows of
seats; she stops one more time and again laughs, looking at
the three who are still on stage; she disappears from the auditorium, and from the lobby her laughter is still heard.
Shortly thereafter the curtain falls.]*

TRANSLATOR'S NOTES

The theater envisaged is of the type most usual where and when the play was written—Italy, 1921. Attempts to substitute a non-Italian type of theater of a later date break down because unless very drastic changes are made in the script, you are still left with items that don't properly fit. You cannot, for example, pretend this is an Off-Broadway theater in 1970 if you then proceed to call a character "Second Actress"—Actor's Equity Association hasn't a single member who would accept the title. With such things in mind, the translator decided simply to translate. And so the reader has the job of imagining a theater he is probably not familiar with—a theater in which, for example, there is a prompter in a prompter's box, center stage.

The second most important personage in the play is called, in the original, Direttore-Capocomico. A Direttore is a managing director or manager. Capocomico one would first be inclined to translate as Actor Manager, and the Actor Managers of the Victorian age did direct the plays. The only trouble here is that Pirandello's Capocomico obviously does not act. He is a Director-Manager, and I think there is, in American English, no alternative to calling him the Director, even though the present-day Italian word for that is Regista. It is a matter of the evolution of this particular profession. The Direttore-Capocomico is an intermediate figure between the old Actor Managers and the new Directors. Pirandello gets to the latter in a later play, *Tonight We Improvise*.

One note on the stage directions. In this play, there are few personal names, so that characters are generally referred to as just *him* or *her*. This forces the author to insert very many parentheses on the pattern of "Pointing to the Father." When possible, the translator has taken the liberty of shortening these to just (to stick to the example) "the Father" in parentheses.

The Italian text followed is that of the *Maschere Nude* as reprinted by Mondadori in 1948. This represents Pirandello's final revision of the play. The translation published in America by the E. P. Dutton Company was based on an earlier Italian text, namely, on the first edition of 1921. The three substantial passages in the first edition which Pirandello cut from his later revisions are included here in footnotes, so that the American reader gets a chance to see what Pirandello's changes amounted to. (No detailed study of *all* the changes has as yet been made, it would seem. The present translator is aware of three different stages of revision: the final version, the second edition [1923], and the first edition [1921].) The Dutton text, by Edward Storer, is literal but often erroneous. There is an accurate, and therefore helpful, translation of the first edition into French by Benjamin Crémieux.

1. *Il giuoco delle parti*, published in English as *The Rules of the Game*.

2. A humble priest in Manzoni's *The Betrothed*.

3. Pirandello gives four lines of the song in French, and hitherto the English translators have followed him. However, the song is an American one, music by Dave Stamper, lyrics by Gene Buck, from the Ziegfeld Follies, 1917. Here are the words:

In a fairy book a Chinese crook
Has won such wondrous fame
But nowadays he appears in plays
And Chu Chin Chow's his name.
With his forty thieves he now achieves

A great success each night.
Just lend an ear and listen here
And I will put you right:
  Beware of Chu Chin Chow!
  Take care, he's coming now!
  He's a robber from the Orient
  And he's filled with Chinese sentiment.
  At night when lights are low
  He wanders to and fro.
  He's the master of his art.
  He can steal a girlie's heart.
  Love he'll plunder, he's a wonder:
  Chu Chin Chow!
Mister Chu Chin Chow you must allow
Has a manner all his own
For he does not woo as others do
He's never quite alone.
With his forty jugs he carries hugs
And kisses to bestow.
'Tis in the sand he'll win your hand,
This Chinese Romeo.
  Beware of Chu Chin Chow, etc.

(Copyright 1917 by T. B. Harms and Francis, Day and Hunter.)

4. The first edition had the Father continue as follows:—"Because, finally, the drama is all in this: when the mother reenters my home, the family she had elsewhere, which was being, as it were, superimposed on the first one, comes to an end, it's alien, it can't grow in this soil. The little girl dies, the little boy comes to a tragic end, the older girl flees. And so, after all the torment, there remain—we three—myself, the mother, the son. And when the alien family is gone, we too find ourselves alien—the one to the other. We find ourselves utterly desolated. As he (pointing to the Son) scornfully said, it's the revenge of the Demon of Experiment which, alas, I carry inside me, a demon that

makes me seek an impossible good, which is what happens when absolute faith is lacking—the faith that enables us humbly to accept life as it is—instead, in our pride, we try to take it over, creating for other persons a reality we consider to be in their line; but sir, it isn't; each of us has his own reality within him, to be respected before God, even when it harms us."

5. In the first edition, a passage follows most of which is found at a later point of the revised text. But this interesting speech of the Son was dropped: "Perform this! ... As if there were any reason! But he (the Father) has found the meaning. As if everyone couldn't find the meaning of anything that happens in this life, *his* meaning, corresponding to *his* presuppositions! (Pause) He complains, this man, of having been discovered *where* he shouldn't have been and doing *what* he shouldn't have been doing—caught in an act which should have remained hidden, outside that reality which he should have sustained for other people. And I? Hasn't he acted in such a way as to force me to discover what no son should ever discover? That father and mother are alive and are man and woman, for each other, outside that reality of father and mother which we give them. For, as soon as this reality is uncovered, our life is no longer tied to that man and that woman except at a single point—one which will only shame them, should we see it!"

6. In Italian rehearsals, traditionally, the prompter reads all the lines a few seconds ahead of the actors until the latter have completely memorized their roles, if indeed they ever do.

7. In the first edition, the following passage occurs here:

FATHER. If you are truly conscious that your reality, on the other hand, your reality in time is an ephemeral and extremely fleeting illusion which you uncon-

sciously invent, today in this way and tomorrow in'
some other way according to cases, according to
conditions and will and feelings which you invent
with the intellect which shows them to you today in
one way and tomorrow ... who knows how: illusions of reality as acted out in that fatuous comedy
of life which does not end, which can not ever end
because, if tomorrow it should end, then good bye,
all is finished.

DIRECTOR. In the name of God, I wish you at least
would stop your philosophizing and let's see if we
might end this play which you people have brought
me! Too much reasoning, too much reasoning, my
dear sir.—You know you almost seem to me a ...
[*He interrupts and looks him over from top to toe*] ... exactly, yes: You introduced yourself here as a—let's
put it this way—as a character created by an author
who decided not to make a play out of you. Correct?

FATHER. That's the simple truth, sir.

DIRECTOR. Cut it out. None of us believes you. Such
things can't be seriously believed, you must know
that. You know what I rather think is going on?
I think that you are adopting the manner of a certain
author whom I particularly detest—let me admit
that—although, unfortunately, I've had to put on
some of his works. I happen to have been rehearsing
one of them when you all came. [*Turning to the Actors*] Think what we gained by the exchange! From
the frying pan into the fire!

FATHER. I don't know, sir, what author you may be alluding to, but believe me, I feel, I feel what I think.
And only those who do not think about what they
feel would say I am just reasoning: they are blind to
their own feelings. I know, I know that many consider such self-blinding much more human, but
the opposite is true, sir, for man never reasons so
much—on or off the point—as when he suffers. He

wants to see the cause of his sufferings, he wants to know who is giving them to him, if this is just or unjust. When, on the other hand, he is enjoying himself, he just accepts the enjoyment and stops reasoning—as if to enjoy oneself were a right. Only the animals suffer without reasoning, sir. Yet put on stage a man who reasons in the midst of his suffering, and everyone will object. But let him suffer like an animal and everyone will say: "Oh, yes, he is human."

DIRECTOR. And in the meanwhile you go on reasoning, huh?

FATHER. Because I suffer, sir. I am not reasoning, I am crying aloud the why and wherefore of my suffering.

Selected Bibliography

Anthologies

Bentley, Eric, ed. *Naked Masks*. New York: E.P. Dutton, 1952.
———, trans. *Pirandello's Major Plays*. Evanston, IL: Northwestern University Press, 1991.

Duplaix, Lily, trans. *Short Stories*. New York: Simon & Schuster, 1959.

Duplaix, Lily, and Frances Keene, trans. *The Merry-Go-Round of Love and Selected Stories*. With a foreword by Irving Howe. New York: New American Library, 1964.

May, Frederick, trans. *Short Stories*. London: Oxford University Press, 1965; 1975; Reprinted London: Quartet Encounters, 1987.

Murray, William, trans. *Pirandello's One-Act Plays*. Garden City, NY: Doubleday Anchor, 1964; New York: Samuel French, 1970; New York: Funk & Wagnalls, 1970.

Ortolani, Benito, ed. and trans. *Pirandello's Love Letters to Marta Abba*. Princeton, NJ: Princeton University Press, 1994.

Rietty, Robert, ed. *Collected Plays*. 3 vols. London: John Calder, 1987, 1988, 1992; New York: Riverrun Press, 1987, 1988, 1992.

Selected Biography and Criticism

Alessio, Antonio, Domenico Pietropaolo, and Giuliana Katz, eds. *Pirandello and the Modern Theatre*. Ottawa: Canadian Society for Italian Studies, 1992.

Bassanese, Fiora A. *Understanding Luigi Pirandello*. Columbia: University of South Carolina Press, 1997.

Bassnett, Susan, ed. *Luigi Pirandello in the Theatre: A Docu-*

mentary Record. University of Warwick, Great Britain: Harwood Academic, 1993.

Bassnett-McGuire, Susan. *Luigi Pirandello*. New York: Grove Press, 1984.

Bentley, Eric. *The Pirandello Commentaries*. Evanston, IL: Northwestern University Press, 1986.

Biundo, James V. *Moments of Selfhood: Three Plays by Luigi Pirandello*. New York: Peter Lang, 1990.

Bloom, Harold, ed. *Luigi Pirandello*. New York: Chelsea House, 1989.

Büdel, Oscar. *Pirandello*. London: Bowes and Bowes, 1966. 2nd ed., 1969.

Cambon, Glauco, ed. *Pirandello: A Collection of Essays*. Englewood Cliffs, NJ: Prentice-Hall, 1967.

Caputi, Anthony. *Pirandello and the Crisis of Modern Consciousness*. Urbana: University of Illinois Press, 1988.

Da Vinci Nichols, Nina, and Jana O'Keefe Bazzoni. *Pirandello and Film*. Lincoln: University of Nebraska Press, 1995.

Di Gaetani, John Louis, ed. *A Companion to Pirandello Studies*. Foreword by Eric Bentley. New York: Greenwood Press, 1991.

Firth, Felicity. *Pirandello in Performance*. Cambridge: Chadwyck-Healey, 1990.

Giudice, Gaspare. *Pirandello: A Biography*. Trans. Alastair Hamilton. London: Oxford University Press, 1975.

Günsberg, Maggie. *Patriarchal Representations: Gender and Discourse in Pirandello's Theatre*. Oxford: Berg, 1993.

MacClintock, Lander. *The Age of Pirandello*. Bloomington: Indiana University Press, 1951.

Matthei, Renate. *Luigi Pirandello*. 1967. Trans. S. and E. Young. New York: Ungar, 1973.

Oliver, Roger W. *Dreams of Passion: The Theater of Luigi Pirandello*. New York: New York University Press, 1979.

Paolucci, Anne. *Pirandello's Theater: The Recovery of the Modern Stage for Dramatic Art*. Carbondale: Southern Illinois University Press, 1974; London: Feffer & Simons, 1974.

Ragusa, Olga. *Luigi Pirandello: An Approach to His Theatre*. Edinburgh: Edinburgh University Press, 1980.

Sogliuzzo, A. Richard. *Luigi Pirandello Director: The Playwright in the Theatre*. Metuchen, NJ: Scarecrow, 1982.

Stone, Jennifer. *Pirandello's Naked Prompt: The Structure of Repetition in Modernism*. Ravenna, Italy: Longo, 1989.